# LITERACY LEARNING CLUBS IN GRADES 4–8

# Best Practices in Action

### Linda B. Gambrell and Lesley Mandel Morrow,
*Series Editors*

Connecting research findings to daily classroom practice is a key component of successful teaching—and any teacher can accomplish it, with the right tools. The Best Practices in Action series focuses on what elementary and middle grade teachers need to do "on Monday morning" to plan and implement high-quality literacy instruction and assess student learning. Books in the series are practical, accessible, and firmly grounded in research. Each title provides ready-to-use lesson ideas, engaging classroom vignettes, links to the Common Core State Standards, discussion questions and engagement activities ideal for professional learning communities, and reproducible materials that purchasers can download and print.

**Teaching Informational Text in K–3 Classrooms:
Best Practices to Help Children Read, Write, and Learn from Nonfiction**

*Mariam Jean Dreher and Sharon Benge Kletzien*

**Reading and Writing in Preschool: Teaching the Essentials**

*Renée M. Casbergue and Dorothy S. Strickland*

**Oral Language and Comprehension in Preschool:
Teaching the Essentials**

*Lesley Mandel Morrow, Kathleen A. Roskos,
and Linda B. Gambrell*

**Literacy Learning Clubs in Grades 4–8:
Engaging Students across the Disciplines**

*Heather Kenyon Casey*

# Literacy Learning Clubs in Grades 4–8

## ENGAGING STUDENTS ACROSS THE DISCIPLINES

### HEATHER KENYON CASEY

Series Editors' Note by
Linda B. Gambrell and Lesley Mandel Morrow

THE GUILFORD PRESS
New York    London

LIMITED DUPLICATION LICENSE

These materials are intended for use only by qualified professionals.

The publisher grants to individual purchasers of this book nonassignable
permission to reproduce all materials for which permission is specifically granted
in a footnote. This license is limited to you, the individual purchaser, for personal
use or use with your students. This license does not grant the right to reproduce
these materials for resale, redistribution, electronic display, or any other purposes
(including but not limited to books, pamphlets, articles, video- or audiotapes,
blogs, file-sharing sites, Internet or intranet sites, and handouts or slides for
lectures, workshops, or webinars, whether or not a fee is charged). Permission to
reproduce these materials for these and any other purposes must be obtained in
writing from the Permissions Department of Guilford Publications.

Library of Congress Cataloging-in-Publication Data is available from the publisher.

ISBN 978-1-4625-2993-3 (paperback)
ISBN 978-1-4625-2994-0 (hardcover)

The NextGenScience logo appears with the permission of NextGenScience.
Its use does not suggest collaboration in or endorsement of the contents of this work.

*For my boys,*
*Ryan, Dylan, Collin, and Shane*

# About the Author

**Heather Kenyon Casey, PhD,** is Associate Professor of Literacy Education at Rider University in Lawrenceville, New Jersey, where she teaches undergraduate and graduate courses in literacy, coordinates the graduate-level literacy concentration, and is Site Director of the National Writing Project. A former middle school language arts teacher and a certified reading specialist, Dr. Casey is past co-chair of the Adolescent Literacy Task Force and the Literacy Reform Task Force of the International Literacy Association (ILA). Her research focuses on the use of collaborative learning structures and new literacies to support adolescent literacy development and engagement. She has published numerous articles and book chapters in these areas and recently coedited a series for the ILA, Literacy Practices That Adolescents Deserve. She has also led several grants in partnership with the National Writing Project focusing on building teacher leadership.

# Series Editors' Note

Like all books in the Best Practices in Action series, *Literacy Learning Clubs in Grades 4–8: Engaging Students across the Disciplines* is grounded in research and situated in appropriate theory for the age group being discussed. From this scholarly beginning, Heather Kenyon Casey clearly describes how to organize and manage literacy learning clubs that support all children in the intermediate and middle grades. Drawing on her deep knowledge of theory, Dr. Casey explains the social-cognitive basis for learning clubs and suggests that in order to fully engage with and enjoy learning, students in grades 4–8 need to be socially involved with others. At the heart of the literacy learning club is the belief that learning is social. This sociocultural view recognizes that learning is dependent on the learner, the text, and the context in which all are situated.

Dr. Casey guides readers through the five components of a successful literacy learning club. First is a focusing session, where the teacher models or demonstrates specific strategies to learn. He or she teaches the children how to work in collaboration with each other and identifies group goals. Second is time for children to gather information and discuss the resources they need to complete their task. Dr. Casey is a believer in multimodal learning. She likes her students to mix the old and the new; she likes digital tools, but also pencil and paper. Before the gathering time, children discuss ways to find materials. During the gathering, children collect resources they need. The third component is the club meetings, which encourage an open exchange of ideas. The teacher spends time teaching children how to collaborate and share their ideas. Fourth is focusing and doing the work.

At this stage, students are enabled to discuss what they learned, how they came to learn the new information, what they are still uncertain about and want to know, and how well they have accessed the information they need. The club work ends with the fifth component, think-alouds, which offer students an opportunity to see inside the teacher's mind as he or she models and demonstrates the literacy habits of a discipline. Think-alouds allow us as teachers to make our thinking explicit in ways that help students understand the literacy steps navigated in a specific disciplinary topic or text.

In her description of the elements needed to carry out a successful literacy learning club, Dr. Casey understands that learning is best understood through a gradual release of responsibility. This model describes learning as a series of carefully scaffolded experiences in which the teacher gradually "lets go" until students are able to work on the skill or concept independently. Literacy learning clubs are a framework but not a script. Within the experience, children have choice. In many classrooms, this is not the case because the experiences provided for children are too heavily mediated by teachers' beliefs about students' needs and by curricular expectations.

Dr. Casey explains how to put the flexible structure of literacy learning clubs into use in language arts, science, social studies, math, and special area classrooms. There are inspiring vignettes throughout of actual learning clubs in operation, plus multiple suggestions for further reading and an appendix rich with sample planning guides and other resources to support teachers and students in starting and managing their own literacy learning clubs.

LINDA B. GAMBRELL, PhD
LESLEY MANDEL MORROW, PhD

# Acknowledgments

I have been fortunate to have had many influential teachers and scholars in my life—my own professional "learning club" that spans decades of listening and learning about literacy.

My professional and personal life has been forever shaped and influenced by Dr. Lesley Mandel Morrow. Our relationship began during my undergraduate years at Rutgers University and continued during my graduate studies, when she became not only a teacher and mentor but a dear friend. Lesley provides a model of how to bridge research, theory, and practice in ways that are transformative. I am grateful for her mentorship of my teaching and scholarship throughout my professional development and for her friendship.

I have the good fortune of having my own family literacy learning club, beginning with my mother and father, John and Joan Kenyon, who shaped my passion for literacy by modeling their own from the time I was young until now. They are and always will be my first and best teachers.

My husband, Jim, and our four incredible boys, Ryan, Dylan, Collin, and Shane, are a daily reminder of what matters most, and their support of my professional pursuits is unwavering. Every day in our family is a fantastic adventure full of love, laughter, learning, and literacy. They are my most treasured literacy learning club.

# Contents

## PART II

# LITERACY LEARNING CLUBS INSIDE THE DISCIPLINES

## PART III

# LITERACY LEARNING CLUBS OUTSIDE THE CLASSROOM

Contents

APPENDIX

Purchasers of this book can download and print enlarged versions
of the materials in the Appendix at *www.guilford.com/casey-forms*
for personal use or use with students (see copyright page for details).

# LITERACY LEARNING CLUBS IN GRADES 4–8

## PART I

# THE RESEARCH, THEORY, AND PEDAGOGY OF LITERACY LEARNING CLUBS

## CHAPTER 1

# Joining the Club

Frank Smith invited us to the literacy club in 1987, and since then membership has grown and changed in ways that he never could have imagined. The participatory culture of the world in which we live invites the ability to work with texts that leap off the page in virtual scenarios and settle into the minds of our emerging adolescents in enduring and enticing ways (Jenkins & Kelley, 2013). Have you seen the excitement of a 10-year-old when he gets to pick the book he is going to read? Or the movie she is going to make? It is not "new news" that emerging adolescents in the upper elementary and middle school grades (4–8) like choice, that they like to hang out and talk with their friends, and that they sometimes do so in ways that keep adults "out of the club." Maybe it is time that we find a way in and use their worlds to open up classroom opportunities for learning and welcome adolescents to the literacy club, the learning club, in this engaging, multimodal world in which we all live. In this text, I will introduce you to many students and teachers who do not reflect any one individual but instead are composite portraits of many of the adolescents and educators I have the good fortune of working with in my own professional life. My literacy learning club.

I am grateful to be writing this text while I have elementary and middle school children of my own. In fact, as I write these opening words, I am mindful of the way new literacy practices weave their way into both their academic and personal lives (O'Byrne & Pytash, 2015). Behind me, my eighth-grade son, Ryan, sits with ear buds in place, watching video clips about landmarks in France on the new school-issued Chromebook that is part of the one-to-one initiative in his school.

While he watches, he takes notes using traditional literacies and will submit a penned summary of these videos—this, after he just created his own "all about me" slide that has been posted to the class set of Google Slides that will encourage an understanding of community in a digital space. He introduced me to his peers and teacher, many of whom I have yet to (and may never) meet in person by scrolling through this shared document.

Dylan, his fifth-grade brother, just completed a traditional math assignment using a digital textbook that required close reading to decode word problems and pencil to demonstrate the solution. He quickly returns to a video game where he interacts with friends through text and image. So much literacy ebbing and flowing in ways that are seamless as these upper elementary and middle school students link their way through their day, drawing on multiple modes for academic and personal purposes (Casey, Lenski, & Hryniuk-Adamov, 2014). As an educator, I am intrigued. What are the classroom bridges that scaffold and mediate literacy development with the multiple modes of reading and writing, comprehending and constructing, available? What is *our role* in helping emerging adolescents navigate these modes?

## Why Literacy Learning Clubs?: Looking Inside What Motivates and Engages Teens and Tweens

*Literacy learning clubs* link principles of motivation and engagement with the developmental trajectories of the emerging adolescent, the "tweens" and "teens" (9–14) growing up in this multimodal world. "Multimodality" is a term used to describe the many modes of communication available. *This is inclusive of digital tools but not limited to these tools* (Casey, 2012a; Kress, 2010; Siegel, 2012). It is perhaps best understood through example. Composing using words only means that the author is working with a single mode of communication. The moment that mode becomes paired with an image to convey meaning, the author is using multiple modes (multimodality) to make meaning and the reader is, in turn, using multiple modes simultaneously to comprehend. This phenomenon in practice is explored in greater detail in Chapter 2.

Research suggests that the grade 4–8 demographic (these 9- to 14-year-old tweens) shows a literacy slump characterized by less interest in reading and writing for pleasure and an increasing dislike of academic tasks (Alvermann, 2013; Anderman, Griesinger, & Westerfield, 1998; Ebert, 2015). The "fourth-grade slump," a widely used (and sometimes misused) term, stems from a study by Chall, Jacobs, and Baldwin (1990), who tracked 30 children from low-income homes. Chall and colleagues found that when these children entered fourth grade, a marked difference in reading was found that was associated with lack of experiences and exposure to more complex vocabulary as they got older. This focused study looked at a specific economic population. The term "fourth-grade slump," however, has been applied widely to refer to the phenomenon shared by educators that marks the upper elementary and middle school grades as the time when many children, regardless of socioeconomic positioning, become disengaged and even disenfranchised from schools. It is also the time when there is an increase in the identification of reading and writing deficits among children, often leading to special education classification. What is the "magic" (or perhaps lack thereof) that explains this sudden shift in fourth grade? Do we really believe that suddenly in fourth grade these challenges manifest themselves? Is this just a rite of passage, or are there things that we as educators can do to support the literacy learning as these tweens and teens transition from childhood to adulthood?

Research demonstrates the need to support the emerging adolescents' literacy development in ways that position this population of kids for success now and in the future (Casey, Lenski, & Hryniuk-Adamov, 2014/2015; Hinchman & Sheridan-Thomas, 2014; International Reading Association [IRA], 2012; Smagorinsky, 2015). A large body of research linking literacy, motivation, and engagement suggests that *yes*, we can and should be doing this, and we can do so in ways that are responsive to the demands of standards, curriculum, and, most importantly, the "tweens" and "teens" we are supporting (Guthrie, 2008; Guthrie, Wigfield, & Klauda, 2012; Lehman & Roberts, 2014; Tovani, 2011; see Figure 1.1).

At the heart of literacy learning clubs is the belief that learning is social. This sociocultural view of learning that informs this text and the formation of these literacy learning clubs recognizes that learning is dependent on the learner, text, and context in which all are situated (Moje, Dillon, & O'Brien, 2000).

In this introductory chapter, I set the stage for exploring the utility of literacy learning clubs throughout the disciplines as *one way* to support literacy development in grades 4–8 that links to principles of motivation and engagement for this population. To set the stage for this paradigm, I begin by describing the theoretical lens that influences this approach and then explore the link between the social and cognitive development of students in grades 4–8 and principles of motivation and engagement. This discussion is followed by an investigation of research-based paradigms for successful collaborative learning experiences. I conclude with an overview of how these pieces inform the development of literacy learning clubs as a strategy for disciplinary learning and literacy development. Each of these pieces is explored in greater detail and connected to discipline-specific practices in the remaining chapters of the book.

The introduction to the widely adopted (though sometimes contested) Common Core State Standards in English Language Arts (ELA) available at *www.corestandards.org/ELA-Literacy,* offers the following core points in the Introduction:

- They demonstrate independence.
- They build strong content knowledge.
- They respond to the varying demands of audience, task, purpose, and discipline.
- They comprehend as well as critique.
- They value evidence.
- They use technology and digital media strategically and capably.
- They come to understand other perspectives and cultures.

The structure of literacy learning clubs gives an opportunity for the real-life application of these real-world skills and clearly links to the closing statement in the Introduction to the Standards, which reads:

Students appreciate that the 21st-century classroom and workplace are settings in which people from often widely divergent cultures and who represent diverse experiences and perspectives must learn and work together. Students actively seek to understand other perspectives and cultures through reading and listening, and they are able to communicate effectively with people of varied backgrounds. They evaluate other points of view critically and constructively. Through reading great classic and contemporary works of literature representative of a variety of periods, cultures, and worldviews, students can vicariously inhabit worlds and have experiences much different than their own.

**FIGURE 1.1.** Common Core State Standards (CCSS) link. Copyright © 2010 National Governors Association Center for Best Practices and Council of Chief State School Officers. All rights reserved.

## Understanding the Sociocultural Lens

When I first began teaching, the notion that *theory* would somehow relate to my own work with children seemed foreign. When I began graduate school as a relatively new seventh-grade teacher and was asked to consider the "theoretical perspective" that described my teaching, I could not answer coherently because in my novice mind theory was something that existed in books but what I was doing every day with kids, that was the heart of it, the practice. In my mind, the two did not intersect at all except in the minds of others who failed to understand what teaching involved.

What I came to learn and what I now talk about with the preservice and practicing teachers I teach at the university level is that theory is at the base of all that we do. It guides the moment-to-moment decisions we make in our daily practice, and it is at the heart of the text we select and reject, the conversations we have with children, even how we design our classroom space. Readers, consider the decisions you make moment to moment, day to day, in your classrooms. There is a pattern and a rhythm to these choices, but a dissonance occurs in our minds as teachers when we are asked to enact a practice that does not align with these decisions, these *theories* of teaching and learning that guide our work with emerging adolescents.

The decision to integrate literacy learning clubs in the emerging adolescents' educational landscape is in direct response to sociocultural perspectives of learning. The sociocultural view, linked to Lev Vygotsky (1896–1934), suggests that learning is social and that it is the mediated interactions with peers that deepen knowledge (Tryphon & Vonèche, 1996; Vygotsky, 1978). Cultural–historical activity theorists (CHAT) took up Vygotsky's work to suggest that when we think of learning it is more than just the one-to-one interactions with others that facilitate learning but also the spaces and places where these interactions take place as well as the artifacts (texts, digital tools, among others) that contextualize these interactions (Bakhtin, 1981). The artifacts that surround learning, such as the texts students create and consume, the classroom design, the peers that surround one another, and the mentoring of the teacher are all part of the experience of *learning*.

Consider, perhaps, the last book club meeting you attended or the productive committee work you engaged in as a participant or leader. Would the outcome have been the same if you had worked in isolation? Did the collaboration with others influence your own perspective and perhaps the outcome? Literacy learning clubs rest on the assumption that in some cases you answered *yes*; the collaboration with others mattered and in fact deepened your own individual understanding in a way that operating in isolation did not. Consider the medical model. Doctors often work in teams to problem solve, learn, and make decisions. So, too, do teams of engineers, mechanics, and others. If this is the world our emerging adolescents are headed toward, why then should school be exclusively individual? Is there room for the collaborative method to not only engage and excite learning but in fact serve as a critical conduit to deeper learning experiences? Putting literacy learning clubs in practice suggests *yes*, there can and should be a place for collaborative literacy experiences across disciplines (Casey, 2012b).

## The Emerging Adolescent

Jasmine is just starting fourth grade and can already see that the expectations will be different. She can now join after-school clubs, and she begins to see that some of her friends are even coming to school with cell phones. At the end of the day, when the school bell rings, in the intermediate wing they can just leave and do not have to wait until an adult greets them at the door. Jasmine can feel things will be different this year, and she is both excited and nervous.

Jasmine's older brother, Elio, is just starting middle school, which in their city begins in seventh grade. Elio now walks to school by himself and even lets himself into the house at the end of the day. He is in charge of his own social plans and loves that he can reach out to friends directly with his cell phone to make plans and just "talk," which occurs mostly via text. Elio enjoys the idea that he can do this outside of his parents' watchful eyes.

Early adolescence is a time of transition—physically, socially, and cognitively. These 9- to 14-year-olds are beginning to explore their own independence in ways that parallel the tremendous changes that infant and early childhood developmental stages offer (Ebert, 2015). Jasmine and Elio, both adolescents at different points in the continuum, share the journey of negotiating independence (Anderman et al., 1998). This change is *developmental,* and from a sociocultural perspective it is contextualized by the environment and experiences that surround them. The sociocultural view of development, in this case adolescent development, suggests that just as two toddlers begin walking at different times, so too do emerging adolescents begin exhibiting these traits along a continuum of time that is influenced by their own cognitive and physical development as well as the experiences that contextualize their lives. The National Middle School Association (NMSA, 2010), in its position paper, *This We Believe: Keys to Educating Young Adolescents,* suggests:

> Every day, millions of diverse, rapidly changing 10- to 15-year-olds make critical and complex life choices and form the attitudes, values, and dispositions that will direct their behavior as adults. They deserve an education that will enhance their healthy growth as lifelong learners, ethical and democratic citizens, and increasingly competent, self-sufficient individuals who are optimistic about the future and prepared to succeed in our ever-changing world. (executive summary)

School should be a place that meets these students where they are and offers learning experiences that reflect their social, emotional, and cognitive development in a way that helps them understand that what they are experiencing *now* in school is preparing them for success later in life.

The emerging adolescent is venturing to make sense of his or her independence academically and socially. It is at this age that, for many adolescents, peer influence increases along with their interest in individualizing their experiences (Baer & Kaufman, 1998; Ebert, 2015). It would be a misrepresentation to offer up the stereotype of the rebellious, difficult tween that is often characterized as disinterested and disengaged. Instead, we need to look beneath that stereotype and consider what the field of early adolescent development can teach us about potential pathways for positively supporting these students.

The field of adolescent psychology offers a compelling portrait of the tween/teen as one who has a heightened interest in peer networks and who is motivated not by the promise of an extrinsic reward but by internal satisfaction (Baer & Kaufman, 1998). Pair this picture with the tendency in many middle schools to limit peer interaction and choice and to offer extrinsic behavioral and academic reward systems and the dissonance is real. Consider what Ryan, an eighth grader, offers as he reflects on his daily work.

> "I like that we have Chromebooks now. It is easier to work on projects in groups because now we don't have to go to the library every time we need to collaborate. We don't even need to be sitting next to one another, but we can still work together. We communicate by e-mail, Google Plus, and now that our teachers have Google Classrooms they can set things up so we can share things with each other. It's way better than trying to figure out a time to get together with all of our crazy schedules. I also like that I can do my work on my own and my teacher can see that but I can also talk to my friends on the classroom pages to get help or to work on group projects."

Dylan, a sixth-grade student at an intermediate school, states:

> "I like that we get to move around more this year when we travel from different classes. It helps my brain not feel tired because I get to move around."

Early adolescents are beginning to consider their relationship to the world in which they live separate from the adults (teachers, parents, etc.) who support them. So what do we need to know about this club to gain access?

While we tend to "box" these changes into arbitrary designations such as physical, cognitive, and social development, the reality is that all three areas are interconnected and occur along a continuum (NMSA, 2010). Those who subscribe to this sociocultural view of development recognize that the notion that learning is social becomes increasingly important for this age group. In addition, opportunities to think more abstractly and to problem solve are characteristic of this demographic (Ebert, 2015; Tryphon & Vonèche, 1996). It is interesting that this time marked by independence socially, emotionally, and cognitively is also characterized by the need for approval and boundaries (Shaw, Amsel, & Schillo, 2011). The adults in the lives of these 9/10- to 14/15-year-olds need to understand this dichotomy when they are building relationships with them and designing learning experiences that positively support their literacy development.

# Motivating and Engaging Literacy Learning
# in Grades 4–8

Chall, Jacobs, and Baldwin's (1990) study that popularized the term "fourth-grade slump" has been generalized to describe the anticipated disengagement of readers and writers when they enter fourth grade. This is not an automatic literacy switch that turns itself off. Instead, it is an acknowledgment that, as children are asked to use literacy to learn discipline-specific content in increasingly complex situations, many of them become disengaged because they are frustrated by texts that are too difficult and that may not seem relevant to their daily experiences (Guthrie, 2008; Kittle, 2013; Miller & Anderson, 2009; Miller & Kelley, 2013; Parsons, Malloy, Parsons, & Burrowbridge, 2015).

This phenomenon, described and highlighted in the popular press, offers many *possibilities* explaining why many early adolescents become disengaged from school. Some educators suggest that the increasing assessment demands have negatively impacted our students and that quite frankly, they are burning out (Tovani, 2011). Others suggest that at a time when early adolescents are seeking increased autonomy and peer collaboration, many of our schools and curriculums are decreasing this autonomy and collaboration in the school spaces (Guthrie et al., 2012). Some believe that first graders are entrusted with more autonomy than these same children are offered as they move into the upper grades, for example. Others criticize the primary grade teachers, suggesting that students are not being given the foundational skills and strategies to use literacy to negotiate the academic disciplines.

The blame game is never helpful in supporting positive change and practice in classrooms. Instead of targeting what is not being done and by whom, we need to consider what motivates and engages early adolescents in light of their developmental needs and to use that as a pathway for carving out instructional strategies and structures that support learning (Abrams & Russo, 2014; Albert, Chein, & Steinberg, 2013). Achieving positive change is not just about the cognitive, social, or physical shifts and demands of early adolescence but rather about understanding the relationship between all of these areas.

## Paradigms at Work in Early Adolescence

There is a large body of research on early adolescent motivation that suggests adolescents are motivated by *choice, success,* and *relevance* (Alvermann, 2013; Casey, 2012a, 2012b, 2012c; Guthrie, 2008). This notion is made manifest in a variety of ways in literacy programs. Book clubs, for example, through which students have the opportunity to select from a menu of texts identified by teachers and then collaborate with peers who have similar interests in discussions and related activities, draw on the belief that learning is social and collaboration is engaging (Daniels, 2002; Harvey & Daniels, 2015). Similarly, lab partners in science classrooms draw on this principle of collaborative investigation and inquiry into relevant and authentic experiences, further demonstrating this theory in practice.

The equation is pretty straightforward. If we want to engage early adolescents in their academic development, their use of literacy to learn, we need to create classroom experiences that are relevant, offer opportunities for independent study as well as collaborative investigation, and trust these students to have some ownership of their ideas. It is interesting that at precisely the time when early adolescents are ready for these kinds of experiences, many curriculums and school configurations are offering more didactic, formulaic learning events that limit collaboration and choice and fail to link in meaningful ways to out-of-class applications.

## Preferred Practices for Collaborative Learning in Grades 4–8

The success of literacy learning clubs is built on the premise that collaborative learning is a positive and productive experience. It is essential, then, that as teachers we understand how to integrate collaboration effectively (Casey, 2012c). The following students and teacher give voice to some of the common misconceptions and concerns that surround collaborative learning:

> "Group work sometimes is confusing. I'm not always sure what I'm supposed to do and usually someone kind of takes over." —Evan, grade 4

> "I hate group work. It's just an excuse for teachers to give lots to do and then I always end up doing it all because I can't usually count on others to help. I like it better when we have individual assignments." —Mandy, grade 6

> "I don't always like group work, but I like it this year in social studies. We each have something we need to do, and then we need to connect it together so it's kind of cool. Plus, we do it all in class so we don't have to try and find a time to meet." —Michael, grade 7

> "I like the idea of kids working together, but I find it really hard to grade so when I have kids in groups I usually don't grade what they are doing." —Ms. S, fifth-grade teacher

Let me be clear: Group work is *not* synonymous with collaborative learning—and therein lies the frustration for many students and teachers. While as educators we are often encouraged to use collaborative learning in our classrooms, we are not often given a clear vision of what it involves. Readers, can you recall a time when you participated in a group activity only to find the bulk of task completion rested on your shoulders? Have you seen that happen in groups of students? Often, that is because we assume that when asked to work together, the tasks will naturally differentiate and individuals will take on a shared piece of the working puzzle. Ms. S, Mandy, Michael, and Evan give voice to the frustration surrounding group activity. Mandy offers some insight. The great irony of the research on effective collaborative learning is that for collaboration to be successful individual accountability and careful structure are key components (Casey, 2012c).

Effective collaborative learning requires the following:

- Limit participation. Four is ideal.
- Assign individuals clearly defined roles, even if the task itself is organic.
- Ensure both individual and group accountability.
- Build in formative assessment for the content studied as well as group efficacy.
- Have teachers serve as facilitators who balance student choice with task goals.

The discipline directs the content, but the collaborative structures that work are consistent.

Consider these two classrooms:

In Mr. Niger's fifth-grade class, he has organized the students into book clubs. He is excited to implement this approach after participating in his own professional book club about this topic. He enthusiastically talks about several historical fiction texts and then groups students according to their preferred text. He is disappointed, however, at the first meeting to see that conversation is slow and the students seem somewhat disengaged. Mr. Niger wonders if this practice is worth the instructional time.

Next door . . .

Mr. Smith also participated in the professional learning community (PLC)with Mr. Niger and is just as excited to implement book clubs with his fifth-grade students. After the students make their initial choices, he conducts mini-lessons on annotating text and on the role of facilitating discussion, and he introduces the kids to the different roles, or lenses, readers assume when they participate in book discussion. These include verifying historical facts, developing discussion points, identifying new concepts, and reading like a writer. This is the first time the class has worked with book clubs, so he assigns specific roles to each meeting; the roles rotate until he feels the conversations no longer need those prescriptions. Mr. Smith is pleased with the way these kids work together and with the thoughtful discussions that take place at each meeting. He plans to implement book clubs again in the near future.

What is the difference between the two experiences? Why has Mr. Niger abandoned the practice and Mr. Smith embraced it? A common misconception is that because emerging adolescents are social, they understand how to engage in professional, academic discourse without teacher guidance. Mr. Smith offers a series of mini-lessons consisting of focused, purposeful, direct instruction that helps his students understand how to productively engage in a book club. Mr. Smith, unlike Mr. Niger, recognizes that it is necessary to heavily scaffold the collaborative experience so that learning occurs (Harvey & Daniels, 2015; Pearson & Gallagher, 1983)

## Connecting the Dots: Informing Literacy Learning Clubs

Multiple intersections of research and theory inform the practice of literacy learning clubs. The purposeful construction of these clubs rests on an understanding of the social, cognitive, and emotional development of youths in grades 4–8, as well as an awareness of the research on motivating and engaging elementary and middle school students. Another key piece of the puzzle consists of the frameworks for effective collaboration in classrooms and the flexible literacy trajectory these tweens and teens navigate. Putting these pieces of the puzzle together allows us to move inside the disciplines so that we can link content and see how transformative literacy learning clubs can be for learning (see Figure 1.2). In this text, I target grades 4–8, though there is certainly utility for this paradigm in the high school setting as well.

This text is organized into three parts. The first part (Chapters 1–3) focuses on the research, theory, and pedagogy of literacy learning clubs. The second part (Chapters 4–8) steps inside the core content disciplines as well as the specialty areas to describe the possibilities literacy learning clubs offer within these content areas. Each of the chapters in Part II includes a section titled "Voices from the Classroom" which offers examples of ways teachers may consider integrating this framework into instruction. These voices echo my daily work with teachers as they

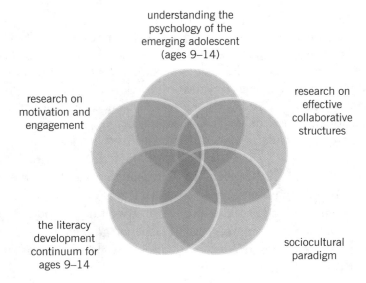

**FIGURE 1.2.** The framework for literacy learning clubs.

work to infuse new practices into instruction. These are composite case studies that draw on my experiences working with many educators and, as such, are built to present the possibilities that literacy learning clubs offer children and teachers. Finally, the last part (Chapters 9–10) looks outward to share ways in which literacy learning clubs can become tools for civic engagement as well as support shared professional study at the school level among teachers. At the conclusion of each chapter are "Questions for Reflection," designed for those readers who choose to engage with this text within their own literacy learning club (see Chapter 10) as well as additional "Activities to Consider."

Readers, as you consider these chapters, I invite you to do what I have done as I wrote the text. Put yourself and your current or future students within these pages and reflect on how pieces of this work might contribute to your ability to support students' learning across the school day while helping developing adolescents create their own cognitive frameworks for learning. The possibilities exist if we are willing to step into the literacy learning club alongside our students. Welcome aboard!

## Summary

The use of literacy learning clubs in grade 4–8 classrooms is linked to a view of learning as social as well as a study of the unique social, emotional, and cognitive

developmental needs in early adolescence. This framework recognizes that invest-
ing in this type of collaborative learning experience requires a deep understanding
of how to build successful collaborations in classrooms. It is crucial that educators
give voice to the theory and research that inform this practice in classrooms in
order to support literacy learning clubs in the classroom as well as adapt as needed
for the contexts specific to each reader of this text.

## QUESTIONS FOR REFLECTION

1. What are some successful experiences you have had with collaborative learning as a
   teacher and/or participant?
2. What learning structures support the students with whom you work? How do you envision the structures described in this chapter supporting learning?
3. Consider your core discipline and/or grade level. Where do experiences such as these
   fit in to the curricular paradigm and opportunities for learning?

## ACTIVITIES TO CONSIDER

- Select a common practice in your classroom. What is the reason you ask students
  to engage in this type of activity? Identify the research base that supports the use of
  this practice in your classroom and prepare to share it with others. In what ways does
  reflecting on this practice influence your continued use of it?

- Interview a colleague in a different discipline and/or grade level. What are some common practices they have adopted? What is the research and/or theoretical rationale for
  these practices? How does this conversation influence your own beliefs about children's
  learning?

## CHAPTER 2

# 21st-Century Membership

Erica, grade 5, wraps up her homework and then quickly moves to her Xbox, where she connects with friends from her class to play a round of Madden16. Ear set on, she is talking and laughing as they play their virtual characters and swap teams as if they were professional coaches.

Raul, grade 8, is offering feedback to his writing partner, real time, via a shared Google doc through the school-issued Chromebook that is part of the new one-to-one initiative at his middle school. As he offers suggestions, his partner responds and does the same for him. This is required homework, and the two have set aside 4:30–5:00 as writing conversation time.

The goal of this chapter is to link the conversation about the theory and practice of successful collaborations for emerging adolescents (Chapter 1) to an understanding of the tools and terms specific to what educators frequently refer to as 21st-century tools. Technology is rapidly transforming academic practices and has the potential to play a significant role in literacy learning clubs. It is important that as educators we understand how to integrate technology in ways that are purposeful and productive and that support adolescent literacy development. The rapid pace at which new tools and applications are unfolding makes this a challenge. New literacy practices remind us that being digitally savvy is not about knowing all of the tools but rather about developing a framework for understanding how digital tools are (or are not) helpful to learning goals. The learning goal *must* remain primary.

Digital tools are integrated into the everyday social lives of teens and tweens and are just beginning to link to the academic practices in the same way. The Pew Research Center reports (Lenhart, 2015) that teens are connected digitally in transformative ways. The data captured in its report indicate a range of social media sites that teens ages 13–17 engage in regularly, with Facebook at the top of the list.

It is difficult to capture these data moment to moment, however. Trends suggest that just as quickly as a new forum for sharing and collaborating evolves, so too do the populations who inhabit these sites. More recent discussions about social media suggest that when some of the parents went to Facebook to monitor their children's interactions, many of these children found other social media outlets to consider, and the trend continues. What we learn from these migrations is that digital tools are providing forums for creating social collaborations designed to be peer–peer, in much the same way the extensive origami-like note folding shared between children prior to these platforms created closed communities. Adolescents enjoy these social collaborations with others. How can we capitalize on that enjoyment in ways that can link to academic experiences?

The Horizon Report (Johnson, Adams Becker, Estrada, & Freeman, 2015) offers a prediction of what the future holds for technology and K–12 education, and as the report makes clear, 21st-century membership provides much richer benefits than simply collecting digital tools. Digital tools are expected to be integrated into the learning cycle in ways that we have yet to imagine. This view that technology is shifting learning and learning structures in fundamental ways suggests that as educators we need to:

- Rethink how schools work.
- Shift to deeper learning approaches.
- Increase the use of collaborative learning approaches.
- Shift from students as consumers to creators.
- Increase the use of blended learning.
- Encourage the rise of STEAM (science, technology, engineering, arts, and mathematics) learning.

There are specific strategies that partially accomplish these goals, such as using technology to locate information or creating a digital-based product as a final assessment. In these cases, technology may be a useful tool as part of a lesson or unit of study. Literacy learning clubs invite the integration of digital tools into the discipline-specific content for both elementary generalists and upper-grade content specialists in ways that support learning that is compatible with how these teens and tweens naturally go about their social lives. This does not mean that literacy learning clubs will fall apart if you do not have access to digital tools for students. Instead, much like we anticipate different print resources supporting and enriching our work, digital tools provide another resource to support these collaborative learning experiences; they can do so in ways that not only support the learning goal but have the potential to transform students' awareness of accessing digital technologies for professional learning purposes.

It is not surprising that 92% of teenagers report going online daily (Lenhart, 2015). Teens, on average, send 30 text messages a day. Among these digital platforms, social media outlets occupy much of the time teens are on the Internet (Lenhart, 2015; see Figure 2.1).

Consider the literacy skills used to compose and comprehend with these digital tools. Composing a text message or a tweet requires the capacity to synthesize information in small units and, in some cases, to condense words into particular sounds. Making use of social media platforms invites a blending of modes of communication (image, word, and sound) in an interactive setting that is highly participatory and in some instances, temporary, as some of these sites allow postings for only a short duration. This invites a wildly different composition and comprehension experience than is possible with traditional paper and pencil and printed texts.

These platforms have largely existed as *social* (hence the name) and separate from the academic experience. As digital tools have become more accessible and integrated into our adult lives, schools, often the last to change, have recognized the necessary role they can play in helping K–12 students understand the utility

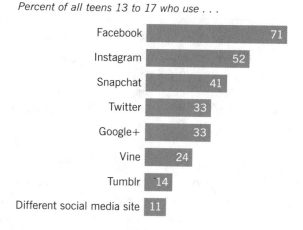

*Percent of all teens 13 to 17 who use . . .*

| | |
|---|---|
| Facebook | 71 |
| Instagram | 52 |
| Snapchat | 41 |
| Twitter | 33 |
| Google+ | 33 |
| Vine | 24 |
| Tumblr | 14 |
| Different social media site | 11 |

**FIGURE 2.1.** Social media platforms for teens. From "Teens, Social Media & Technology Overview 2015," Pew Research Center, Washington, DC (April 2015). Reprinted by permission.

of these tools and develop the critical reasoning and literacy skills needed to successfully navigate across these spaces. When I work with preservice and practicing teachers who are integrating digital tools into instruction (first it was iPads, then Chromebooks; remember when AOL was the only e-mail provider?), I don't talk about learning the specific platforms that are always shifting and changing but instead consider what these perpetually shifting tools and platforms require of readers and writers.

Future projections suggest that in the immediate future classrooms will be populated with the opportunity to BYOD (bring your own devices) and makerspaces. Makerspaces, which grew out of work in media centers and libraries, invite students to use discarded resources to create new objects. This phenomenon excites creative problem solving and supports critical thinking as students imagine new possibilities. The use of digital tools to share these creations for feedback via social networks and their use within the creations themselves are creating opportunities for individual exploration to be mediated by both face-to-face and virtual collaboration (Norris, 2014). While this approach does not require 21st-century technologies, it is being seen as a way to develop the cognitive framework necessary for success in our rapidly evolving 21st century. Soon, 3D printing and adaptive learning technologies are expected to populate the schools and eventually to be superseded by digital badges and wearable technology (Johnson et al., 2015). Although these are predictions, the rapid way in which technology is infiltrating our lives generally and our learning in schools specifically suggests that these tools can support students' literacy development, which is essential to making them college, career, and life ready.

Larry Page of Google describes this as "10X" thinking. This approach suggests that learning occurs when participants are asked the right questions and are given the opportunity to "mess around" through inquiry-based experiences (Levy, 2013). This concept, applied to the classroom, creates opportunities to problem solve across classes and across content and allows our tweens and teens to gain knowledge while building independent frameworks for learning. *Literacy is the pathway through which this learning occurs.* The collaborative framework implicit within the literacy learning clubs provides the context that makes this learning possible.

A middle school principal I work with recently said to a group of parents at Back to School Night, "Our kids use technology like we breathe air." Many of the teachers I work with, feeling a bit out of breath themselves, wonder if they can "keep up," the way the next generation (often referred to as "digital natives") can (Prensky, 2001). Entering that race is not helpful. New technology is emerging rapidly. For example, in a recent Pew report that surveyed technology experts about projections for the future, Anderson and Rainie (2014) found that experts foresee an ambient information environment where accessing the Internet will be effortless and most people will tap into it so easily it will flow through their lives "like electricity." They predict mobile, wearable, and embedded computing will be tied together in the Internet of Things, allowing people and their surroundings to tap into artificial intelligence-enhanced cloud-based information storage and sharing (1).

This view calls for educators to help students understand how to integrate and adapt these tools that are becoming embedded in our personal and professional lives. Teaching the tools themselves only begins to scratch the surface. It is a bit like teaching students to memorize effective essays instead of helping students learn how to structure their own within a variety of genres. It is about teaching students how to *think* with technology, not just *use* the tools.

This calls for an imperative to look beyond the specific tools and platforms and examine the reading and writing strategies needed to use digital tools successfully for academic purposes (Hinchman & Sheridan-Thomas, 2014; Turner & Hicks, 2015). We also need to consider how the (relatively) free and open access that the World Wide Web offers creates opportunities for readers and writers to engage in interactive composition and comprehension. Doing so allows us to build students who truly are college and career ready as we prepare them for a world where digital technologies are integrated into every facet of their personal and professional lives. Our job as educators, then, is to scaffold the strategies needed to make use of these tools productively and successfully for academic purposes (Turner & Hicks, 2015).

Let us explore what is intended when we throw ideas around such as *new literacy practices*, *multimodality*, and *digital tools and platforms*, so that we will have a common language to explain how these constructs are influencing activities in upper elementary and middle grade classrooms. What do we mean when we reference these ideas and practices, and how can it help us prepare emerging adolescents for success in the 21st and 22nd centuries?

## Multimodality

Multiple methods (or modes) are available to communicate information—the written word, a drawing, a snapshot, a video. Each of these modes by itself conveys information. When modes are paired and woven together in an effort to convey information, we have ventured into multimodality (Kress, 2010). Multimodality is often seen as a new phenomenon because of the preponderance of blended words and images that technology invites. The idea of integrating various communication approaches is not new, however. At the time of the printing press (1400s), the idea of linking image with word offered a newer type of literacy experience than had previously been available (Coiro, Knoble, Lankshear, & Leu, 2008). It was the "new literacy" of the time period. Fast forward several hundred years and the "new literacy" is the access to technology and the Internet. Think of the last time you searched for something on the Internet. It probably yielded a collection of images, words, and resources that paired many modes you needed to synthesize in order to understand the results of the query. The National Council of Teachers of English (NCTE, 2013) offers this definition of 21st-century literacy in its position statement:

> Literacy has always been a collection of cultural and communicative practices shared among members of particular groups. As society and technology change, so does literacy. Because technology has increased the intensity and complexity of literate environments, the 21st century demands that a literate person possess a wide range of abilities and competencies—many literacies. These literacies are multiple, dynamic, and malleable. As in the past, they are inextricably linked with particular histories, life possibilities, and social trajectories of individuals and groups. Active, successful participants in this 21st-century global society must be able to
>
> - Develop proficiency with the tools of technology;
> - Build intentional cross-cultural connections and relationships with others so as to pose and solve problems collaboratively and strengthen independent thought;
> - Design and share information for global communities to meet a variety of purposes;
> - Manage, analyze, and synthesize multiple streams of simultaneous information;
> - Create, critique, analyze, and evaluate multimedia texts;
> - Attend to the ethical responsibilities required by these complex environments.

Helping adolescents understand how to integrate modalities (both the new and the traditional) is an essential part of literacy development. The CCSS recognizes the necessity of blending these modes within and across disciplines and genres in the English language arts (ELA; National Governors Association Center for Best Practices & Council of Chief State School Officers [NGA & CCSSO], 2010). The International Literacy Association (formerly the International Reading Association) also supports the idea that literacy development requires building the capacity to work across and within the varied types of text that are inclusive of print and fixed and moving visuals to construct and comprehend meaning (IRA,

2009). The ILA's position statement on adolescent literacy offers the following call to action for those of us working with the upper elementary and middle school demographic:

> More than ever, adolescents need teachers who can help them understand how to read and interpret texts critically and to position themselves strategically as authors in a Web 2.0 environment. Specifically, instruction is needed that will enable students to comprehend and construct a range of multimodal texts across genres, disciplines, and digital spaces. Teaching comprehension and composition, while always a mainstay of the school curriculum, is even more crucial today. Likewise, the stakes have never seemed higher for teaching students to think critically about what they see, hear, view, and construct in the relatively untamed world of Web 2.0. (p. 8)

Multimodality is perhaps best understood through example (see Figure 2.2). It is the strategic use of at least two text modes that may serve a variety of purposes that are inclusive of conveying information, sharing stories, arguing a position, or a blending of these and more across the literacy continuum.

Advertisements are often a straightforward way of understanding how this works. Viewing a television advertisement without the music or voice-over, and vice versa, demonstrates the power of this integration (Casey, Lenski, & Hryniuk-Adamov, 2014/2015). Another classroom example that is gaining momentum is the use of video trailers as a way to demonstrate comprehension of text or topic using short documentaries. The accessibility of the tools to capture and construct these images is inviting their increased use in the classroom and with that, comes

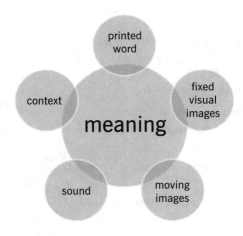

**FIGURE 2.2.** Multimodality.

the necessity to help students understand how to work with these digital tools critically and responsibly. Consider this exchange in a recent staff meeting of fifth- to eighth-grade teachers who are piloting a one-to-one Chromebook initiative:

> As the teachers settle in for additional professional development on the new Chromebooks there is a bit of unrest in the back. "Why are we here again?" is heard by the presenter. "The kids know how to use these. It's just about putting online the stuff we used to photocopy. This whole initiative is more about saving paper than anything else."

Engaging with digital tools without reflecting on how the tool is influencing learning is dangerous for youth and adolescent literacy development. "Going green" only scratches the surface of the value of integrating digital tools into learning. The students we work with, these digital natives (Prensky, 2001), may be more comfortable with accessing digital tools, but they need skilled educators to help them develop their ability to analyze and reflect on *how* these tools are supporting understanding. Just as we understand the need to introduce students to discipline-specific text structures, so too do we need to help build a schema for ways of comprehending and composing across digital structures and domains. Technology is not an add-on that involves *doing* in classrooms; it is *shaping* how learning happens.

## New Literacies for New Learning

### Social Media

Research on youth and adolescent use of social media suggests that the majority of adolescents are using some type of social media platform and that the venues are growing (Lenhart, 2015). There are socioeconomic differences. The Pew survey demonstrates that middle- and high-income teens are more likely to use Snapchat, while those from lower socioeconomic backgrounds are more inclined to find themselves on Facebook. The breakdown across gender is interesting, too, as adolescent girls are more likely to use visual social media platforms while boys connect more through games. See the breakdown of these groups in Figure 2.3.

The use of these tools begins early (Madden, Lenhart, Duggan, Cortesi, & Gasser, 2013) and has become a "hot topic" in the popular press and among parenting circles. CNN partnered with child development specialists in #*Being 13: Inside the Secret World of Teens* and discovered that "most adolescents with access to smart phones are living their social lives online as much as they do face to

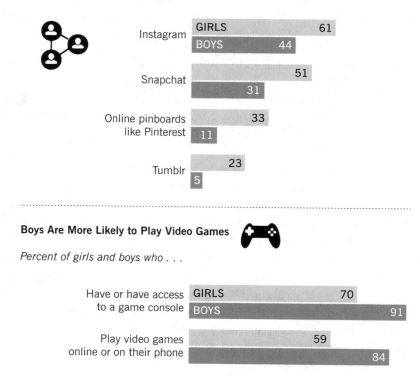

**Girls Dominate Visually-Oriented Social Media Platforms**

*Percent of girls and boys who use . . .*

Instagram — GIRLS 61, BOYS 44

Snapchat — 51, 31

Online pinboards like Pinterest — 33, 11

Tumblr — 23, 5

**Boys Are More Likely to Play Video Games**

*Percent of girls and boys who . . .*

Have or have access to a game console — GIRLS 70, BOYS 91

Play video games online or on their phone — 59, 84

**FIGURE 2.3.** Gender differences in the use of technology. From "Teens, Social Media & Technology Overview 2015," Pew Research Center, Washington, DC (April 2015). Reprinted by permission.

face. Adults worry that teens are hooked on social media, but most have no idea what teens are actually doing online" (Underwood & Faris, 2015). This study has started conversations about digital citizenship and the linking of the literacies used to access these sites with links to academic learning. What is our responsibility in the schools?

In my work with developing and practicing teachers, I have found a range of responses that, interestingly, are not divided across "young" and "old" as might be expected. There is concern that with the existence of relatively benign sites such as the Pacific Northwest Tree Octopus (*http://zapatopi.net/treeoctopus/*) and dihydrogen monoxide (DHMO; *www.dhmo.org/*) or more troubling sites such as *www. martinlutherking.org*, inviting this tool into academic learning will confuse content understanding and literacy development. The first two examples (the Pacific

Northwest Tree Octopus and DHMO) are intentionally designed to motivate critical thinking when interacting with the website, and the third seeks to manipulate viewers, predicated on a platform of hate and bigotry. The opportunities afforded by the Internet and many of these digital tools and platforms calls for an urgent sense of responsibility to help our next generation of digital citizens develop the skill to navigate this wide-open web skillfully and thoughtfully. Where is that skill best taught? I suggest that it is within the safety and security of the classroom with expert modeling by educators. Each of those websites, for example, becomes a powerful opportunity to model expert thinking when navigating information on the Internet. Educators can demonstrate to students how to reveal the layers of meaning within web-based information, just as we often do when working with printed text.

## Accessing and Constructing Information

So what is happening in classrooms that invite new literacies for new learning? As we step inside these spaces, I invite you to consider what learning is occurring and evaluate the effectiveness.

> Mr. W, who teaches in a self-contained fifth-grade class, is getting ready to launch a social studies unit on the American colonies. He decides that instead of the traditional textbook study, he is going to connect this to language arts and read a series of leveled texts. He wants to encourage his students to do active research, so he bookmarks a Google page with useful websites and expects the students to work in pairs to identify three facts to share with the class. Mr. W is discouraged by what they find online and, upon reflection, decides that a text study would have been more effective.

Many of us have found ourselves in this position when we integrate something new into an established curriculum. For Mr. W, it is not that the websites were inaccurate or lacking; rather, it is that he enacted best practice in every aspect of this activity except for the use of technology. This is a common challenge. Mr. W has identified leveled texts to satisfy the needs of the readers; he is drawing on collaborative learning because he knows it is engaging, but he fails to provide the explicit instruction in how to read websites. In addition, he assumes that all students will access all of the websites. This is the same mistake we make when we assign students to leveled guided reading groups but then expect all of them to comprehend equally the same science or social studies text. There are specific strategies for accessing and reading websites that need to be part of our instruction, and students' individual levels of literacy abilities need to be considered. Research documents the disparity between online and offline comprehension, and that is largely due to the fact that the genre exits but the specific strategies for accessing online content are not uniformly part of the curriculum (Leu et al., 2015). Leu, Zawilinski, Forzani, and Timbrell (2014) caution educators to consider the following reality:

> We live during a time in which new technologies continuously appear online, requiring additional skills to effectively read, write, and learn, sometimes on a daily basis. Consider, for example, just a few of these new technologies: Twitter, Facebook, Google+, Siri, Foursquare, Dropbox, Skype, Chrome, iMovie, Contribute, or any of many, many mobile "apps" and ebooks. Each requires additional reading and/or writing skills to take full advantage of its affordances. In addition, new tools for literacy will appear on the Internet tomorrow with additional, New Literacies required to use them effectively. Finally, each online tool regularly is updated; each time this happens new affordances appear, requiring additional skills and strategies. It is clear that the nature of literacy regularly and continuously changes in online spaces. (p. 344)

So what does this mean for classroom instruction? Students need to understand both how to access the tools we integrate and how to evaluate the material found online.

Research on students' work in online spaces suggests that it is tightly tied to problem solving (e.g., Mr. W's query to learn three facts about the colonies) and connected to writing. Before students can read online, they need to find information online. That means developing an understanding of search functions and distilling queries into key words. If we are using specific applications such as microblogging (e.g., Twitter) or blogs (e.g., kidblogging) or social media platforms (e.g., Edmodo, an educational platform similar to Facebook), we need to point out the text features of each to kids. Perhaps we need to integrate strategies such as the following:

- Pair a web-based text with a traditional text and model how you read each differently.
- Identify the text features specific to the web pages (i.e., the headers that also act as hyperlinks and the moving image boxes that often contain advertisements or additional information).
- Model through a think-aloud on how using hyperlinks to work through an Internet document requires a circular type of reading since there is no finite beginning and end as there is for a traditional text.

- Invite students to engage in using these digital tools. Just as in traditional literacies, with online material the reading and writing connection deepens understanding of both.
- Consistently model responsible and safe digital practices in an effort to build mindful Internet consumers and producers.

The CCSS explicitly addresses the need to attend to these strategies across disciplines (NGA & CCSSO, 2010):

> To be ready for college, workforce training, and life in a technological society, students need the ability to gather, comprehend, evaluate, synthesize, and report on information and ideas, to conduct original research in order to answer questions or solve problems, and to analyze and create a high volume and extensive range of print and nonprint texts in media forms old and new. The need to conduct research and to produce and consume media is embedded into every aspect of today's curriculum. (p. 4)

These digital tools support collaboration within literacy learning clubs because they invite connection, and in doing so they meet the objectives outlined above. Consider, for example, the recent rise of Google Documents and Google Classroom. The relatively easy access to Google Documents permits sharing and collaborating virtually. Student groups, along with their teachers, as we saw in the opening scenario, can all be "meeting" from different places, and this can be both synchronous and asynchronous. There are other applications (e.g., Edmodo) that facilitate this type of integration, and if the trends continue more will likely follow.

I am reminded of the weekly digital chat with their science teacher to which a class of seventh graders has access, providing an opportunity for content reinforcement and enrichment along with the building of relationships. Many of these digital tools available for classroom collaboration also allow users of the documents to identify the individual collaborations as well as to view edits over time. This resource creates an immediate accountability that is often missing in the paper-and-pencil group project completed outside of the teacher's view and allows connections in ways that face-to-face meetings do not facilitate. The possibilities are just now being realized in schools. Literacy learning clubs are grounded in the value of collaboration, and these digital tools, by allowing for this type of connection, expand how it can support students' learning across disciplines.

As we move into Chapter 3, we begin to examine the specific components of building literacy learning clubs in grade 4–8 classrooms. I invite you to read the chapter through the lens of how our examination of the theory and research of collaborative inquiry, alongside the potential of 21st-century tools and opportunities, may help you adapt this approach in your own classroom. What pieces of it are already relevant to your current and planned practice? What components might you build that will positively support your students' literacy development and access content understanding? Creating opportunities in schools to support "college and career readiness" and I would add, *life readiness,* requires that educators understand preferred classroom practices that are firmly grounded in research and theory along with the 21st-century digital tools and methodologies that are woven into every facet of all of our lives. Literacy learning clubs offer one structure to support this endeavor.

## Summary

We cannot address literacy learning clubs as a tool for adolescent literacy learning without considering the digital world in which these adolescents live. The participatory environment that is supported by social media, digital tools, and the Internet are becoming an increasingly essential component of literacy education as we work to prepare students for success in their adult lives in the 21st and 22nd centuries. This requires moving away from a *how to* model of understanding specific tools and technologies toward developing a cognitive framework that allows students to examine the utility of tools and integrate in ways that support learning goals. This is a sophisticated task and one that requires careful and thoughtful scaffolding. As we move into examining the key components of literacy learning clubs, it is important to understand how 21st-century tools can be a supportive piece of this process.

## QUESTIONS FOR REFLECTION

1. What access do you and your students have to digital tools in the classroom? What concerns and excites you about the possibilities for student learning?

2. Where can you begin or continue to provide explicit instruction in how to navigate digital technologies in ways that support learning goals? What is needed for you to do so?

## ACTIVITIES TO CONSIDER

- Review your curriculum and lessons. Where can you integrate technology (or continue to do so) in a way that supports the idea that new literacies are about creating a framework for understanding *how* technology can support learning and not an examination of the tool itself. Try a lesson, or a unit of study, or a focused mini-lesson where you think-aloud on one of these principles. What do you find? How is it influencing student learning?

- Survey your grade level/department about students' use of technology. What are you noticing? Are the trends consistent with the data presented here?

## CHAPTER 3

# Literacy Learning Clubs in Action

The literacy learning club is a pedagogical structure that links the belief that adolescent literacy learning can be social (Chapter 1) with the demands of 21st-century literacy practices (Chapter 2). In this chapter, I take a look inside the structure by describing the paradigm itself. While the paradigm for literacy learning clubs is relatively consistent across content areas, academic language and discipline-specific literacy needs must be considered when integrating this structure into the various subject areas. These pieces of the puzzle that describe one pathway for engaging the learner and supporting learning may be configured differently depending on the content studied (Casey, 2012c). In later chapters, I map this structure into specific disciplines with the specific disciplinary literacy lenses in mind. The appendix offers a variety of resources that may be helpful for teachers considering implementing this paradigm into the classroom.

## Connecting the Dots: What Are the Nuts and Bolts of Organizing a Literacy Learning Club?

### Getting Started

Literacy learning clubs can be broken down into five components: (1) focusing session, (2) gathering time, (3) club meeting, (4) focusing finish, and (5) think-aloud (see Figure 3.1). This paradigm evolved out of research in upper elementary and middle school classrooms that considered how different pedagogical structures,

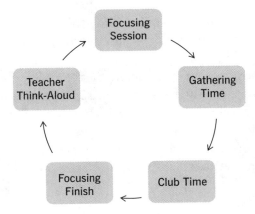

**FIGURE 3.1.** Components of literacy learning clubs. Literacy learning clubs, as presented here, can be understood as a linear progression beginning with focusing time, moving to gathering time, continuing on to club time, transitioning to a focused finish, and concluding with a teacher think-aloud. In many cases, that linear progression makes sense for supporting student learning. It would be an oversimplification of the learning process, however, to assume that facilitated learning always follows this linear progression. Instead, it is more useful when looking across disciplines to understand that these are core pieces of the learning puzzle that can be reconfigured to best suit the goals of the discipline or task.

rooted in the belief that learning is social, engaged adolescents in the content of study and motivated them to participate (Casey, 2012a, 2012b). The time invested varies and can be adjusted based on the needs of the classroom and/or discipline, but it generally falls within 40–60 minutes. As students move through the session(s), learning happens because students interact collaboratively with new ideas in ways that allow individual understanding to occur.

This framework draws on the understanding that learning is best understood through the gradual release of responsibility model (Pearson & Gallagher, 1983). This model describes learning as a series of carefully scaffolded experiences in which the teacher gradually "let's go" until students are able to work on the skill or concept independently. When talking with preservice teachers, I often compare this academic descriptor to learning to walk or ride a bike. The adult holds on less and less until the child is walking or riding independently. While the model is sometimes represented as a linear progression, it is perhaps more useful to consider Fisher and Frey's discussion. These researchers reference the need for focused, direct instruction, collaborative inquiry, and independent application as part of the learning cycle, with an understanding that these elements do not necessarily take place in a set order; instead, they are necessarily recursive in a way that expects learners to return for more support even after they have "let go" so that they can deepen their understanding (Fisher & Frey, 2008). The child who takes a first step may need to return to hand holding the next day before true independence occurs. The adult's hand is there when the child returns, just as the teacher's academic support should be.

This is particularly true, for example, in science and math education, where at the onset, inquiry-based learning resists a focused, explicit mini-lesson. So, while the model is represented here, the ways in which it is enacted needs to be carefully aligned with the skills specific to the disciplines in which the literacy learning club is used. Literacy learning clubs are a *framework*, not a script. The successful integration of literacy learning clubs into the classroom is dependent on the educator's professional ability to adjust, modify, and adapt in order to suit the unique context in which he or she is situated.

The success of the literacy learning club model, like the book club model that this approach follows, stems from the research on adolescent motivation that highlights *choice* as key to student engagement (Guthrie et al., 2012; Harvey & Daniels, 2015). Choice in the classroom is often heavily mediated by teachers' beliefs about students' needs and curricular expectations. For example, when introducing book clubs in a language arts classroom, students are generally choosing from a menu that is established by the classroom curriculum (Daniels, 2002). The recent interest in "genius hour" and "makerspaces," a time when students investigate *anything* of interest, employs the notion that when students are guided by their own curiosity opportunities for teachers to facilitate and guide learning occur. This type of facilitated learning may allow for an even greater level of choice, because students drive content (Fleming, 2015; Juliani, 2014). There are varying degrees of choice that can exist in classrooms. Some, like book clubs, are bound by the curriculum and others such as "genius hour" and "makerspaces" are driven primarily by student interest. Choice, whether bounded or unbounded, has consistently been shown to motivate students. The key is to carefully tie the literacy learning club experience with the objectives of the discipline and unit of study.

When implementing literacy learning clubs in any discipline, teachers first need to identify the balance between student choice and teacher direction. For example, in previous work I did with a sixth-grade health unit (Casey, 2012a), the classroom teacher and I integrated the literacy learning club paradigm to revitalize a unit on body systems. In our work, instead of a survey of all of the systems, the students became expert in one, using the literacy learning club paradigm to develop this expertise, and then they shared this knowledge with their classmates. Choice was limited to the required curriculum's study of specific body systems. Student test data and teacher report suggested a higher understanding of the systems and greater engagement throughout. The teacher and I developed protocols for creating artifacts that would allow their peers to understand the system that they investigated in detail. In this example, student choice was shaped by the menu of options dictated by the curriculum.

In another study, I worked with fourth- and fifth-grade children in an after-school program in which the children identified topics they were interested in learning more about (Casey, 2012b). I did not go in with a specific curriculum or menu; instead, the topics investigated were dictated by student interest. In both cases, the literacy learning club platform was used to guide investigating and learning, but the degree of student choice was different. In both instances, students were highly engaged, supporting the research showing that even when choice is bounded by curricular expectations, engagement is heightened (Harvey & Daniels, 2015; Juliani, 2014). (See the Appendix for sample materials used with students.)

While learning clubs in their truest form allow student choice (whether bounded or open) to determine group composition, teacher mediation may be necessary in the organization of the groups themselves. Upper elementary or middle school teachers understand that the chemistry of group composition is as important as the content to be learned (Casey, 2012c; Garrett, 2014). The unit of study and/or discipline may require an understanding of group chemistry as well as content (Albers, 2012). Literacy learning clubs should support the many ways in which differentiation needs to be implemented to support student learning (Tomlinson, 2001). Key to all of this is the flexibility to identify topics and organize membership based on the learning objectives. That careful alignment is necessary for success. Questions to consider when implementing literacy learning clubs include the following:

"How much time can I devote to these investigations?"
"Do I want the students to identify topics of study, or am I selecting topics from the curriculum?"
"What are my expectations and/or the expectations of my school/district for assessing student learning?"
"What goals do I have for my students? How are these tied to curricular expectations?"
"What types of accountability do I expect from students to demonstrate learning?"

## Focusing Session

The goal of the focusing session is to define the purpose of the learning. For those teachers comfortable with the workshop approach, this closely parallels the mini-lesson. During this time, the teacher generally organizes the learning experience for the session. This orienting session can take any number of directions and generally lasts about 10 to 15 minutes but can be adjusted based on the needs of the discipline or grade level. Topics of focus during this teacher-directed portion of the meeting include, but are not limited to:

- Modeling or demonstration of specific strategies.
- Management needs for a course of study.
- The role of collaborative inquiry to work toward a learning goal.
- Modeling or demonstration of craft.
- Identification of group or class goals.
- Strategies needed to represent or understand discipline-specific content.

The focusing session is perhaps best understood through example.

Ms. Fischer gathers her 24 fifth graders to the front of the interactive white board. The students are getting ready to launch their multimodal persuasive compositions, which are a required unit of study in the fifth-grade language arts curriculum. Ms. Fischer has several learning goals for her students during this extended study:

- To develop the ability to identify persuasive tools when reading print and nonprint text.
- To develop the ability to compose persuasive text using print and nonprint media.

This is Ms. Fischer's first time working with literacy learning clubs, so she only placed two items (pro and con) on the "menu" and chose to work with a curricular-based persuasive topic that, in the past, students investigated independently and then produced a written paper (typed or handwritten). Being new to this pedagogical model, Ms. Fischer is cautious. She elects to work with a topic that is clearly connected to the curricular research and writing goals and one with which she is quite comfortable. There are six groups in the classroom, three of whom are focusing on the benefits of year-round schooling and three of whom are discussing the value of the 10-month system with summers "off." Today's focusing session is designed to help students work with the tool to create a structure around the content.

In this 10-minute modeling session, Ms. Fischer offers specific items for students to consider beyond the tool to document their position. This includes the use of persuasion through a digital documentary when compared to a still image with accompanying text. In doing so, Ms. Fischer models both form and content in an effort to help students understand how both are integrated when working as writers. This focused modeling is needed for the students to make productive and effective use of their club time.

## Gathering Time

During gathering time, which generally takes between 5 and 10 minutes, students identify and collect the resources that are inclusive of texts (both traditional and digital) as well as specific tools that may be discipline-specific (e.g., materials for testing in science, measuring tools in math) needed to investigate the group topic of study. During this time, the teacher facilitates the identification of resources, and the group members begin their collaborative learning experience by determining *together* what is needed and then working to secure the resources. This may include:

- Identifying traditional print materials needed and bringing them to the group.
- Locating and linking electronic platforms as needed.
- Bookmarking useful sites to investigate.
- Organizing material resources needed.
- Ensuring that any necessary digital sources are available.
- Making use of the indices and search functions to identify specific areas of the digital and print text that will be useful to accomplish the group goal.

In Ms. Fischer's class, after she models different persuasive techniques and strategies, the groups spend a few minutes considering the types of resources that might help them achieve their goal of creating a multi-modal text that signals their position on the topic selected. Next, each member of the group is charged with locating at least one resource, either print or digital, from the materials provided. Ms. Fischer, in collaboration with the media center specialist, has put together a traditional library "cart" with books and magazines that focus on the history of school. Each of these texts includes a section on how schools are organized and why that organization was selected.

In addition, the class also has access to a set of Chromebooks they can use to identify additional resources that include video and websites about schools, as well as current data about how many schools nationally are reconfiguring their school calendars to reflect social shifts and needs. Ms. Fischer has bookmarked a number of sites in anticipation of students' research needs. She asks students to use a mix of both resources so that she can be confident that her students are learning the necessary skills to negotiate both print and nonprint materials. As students are busy pulling materials from the cart and bookmarking potential digital resources in their "favorites folder," Ms. Fischer circulates, facilitates, and mediates to help students understand how to secure useful resources. Ms. Fischer's role has clearly shifted as the class moves from direct instruction to facilitated collaborative learning (Fisher & Frey, 2008).

## Club Meeting

The club meeting is the heart of the collaborative experience. During the club meeting, students actively engage with the content they are investigating, using the multiple information sources identified during gathering time to deepen their learning. The club meeting time is predicated on the understanding that learning is social and that through open exchange individual students begin to anchor understanding and deepen learning in a way that engaging with information in isolation does not allow.

These open exchanges become purposeful and successful when students are offered focused instruction on how to interact and engage in these environments. Teachers sometimes abandon small-group activities because they have had experiences of students being off task and unproductive when engaged in collaborative inquiry (Casey, 2012c). The irony of successful collaborative experiences is that teachers need to carefully scaffold and model how to engage effectively and purposefully in these types of experiences if they are going to be productive. It is the absence of this modeling and expectation that often creates a failed collaborative experience. Successful small-group collaborations happen because teachers have carefully structured and mediated the experience. It is so much more than simply putting kids in groups and expecting learning to occur. Much of this learning may occur during the focusing session when time is spent on modeling and identifying effective group participation. Teachers can continue to support effective collaboration when they circulate and facilitate these group exchanges. For example, during club time students may:

- Work individually with a specific resource for a determined amount of time and then come together to share what was found and synthesize how these findings contribute to the essential questions/topic guiding the learning.
- Begin with shared investigation and then break off into either partnerships or individual exploration, with an understanding of what either the partnership or the individual is accountable for when reporting back to the group.

Protocols may be needed to help students discuss content such as:

- "What can we learn from this text/resource I am investigating?"
- "How does that connect with what my colleagues (scientists, social scientists, readers, etc.) have identified in their group?"

Critical to this club time is the useful exchange of ideas in an effort to deepen understanding. Learning can be uncomfortable, so this time may result in feelings of confusion and uncertainty as students engage in content that is new and unfamiliar. For example, in an algebra class, students involved in learning clubs may be working with equations as a way to understand economic impact and may be uncertain and uncomfortable about what they are coming to learn as they work with the math to connect to content. This is a welcome experience because it is through this exchange of ideas and even this discomfort that they may begin to understand the content in ways that simply moving through the equations may not allow. In previous research, this period of discomfort was identified as crucial to the student learning experience (Casey, 2012a, 2012b).

When I first began integrating literacy learning clubs into classrooms, I was reminded of the importance of allowing students to work through challenge and to avoid the pull to immediately rescue students from moments of discomfort and frustration. This was (and is) a necessary step in learning (Shanahan, 2015). As teachers, one of the things we often feel the need for is more *time*, particularly during this era of increasing expectations around standards and high-stakes assessment, but I suggest that it is in this cognitive negotiation, this attempt to *make sense* of the new, that learning happens. This is *not* to be confused with asking students to work for prolonged periods of time at their frustration level.

The increasing use of digital sources to support learning works well in this paradigm. While students can certainly work primarily with traditional texts and resources, the rise of one: one initiatives in schools provides a natural forum for collaboration with individual accountability. The use of Google Documents to collaborate, while offering an individual footprint, allows teachers to understand how individuals connect and answers the challenging question of understanding individual contributions in collaborative endeavors.

As a teacher, for example, I can review a Google Document or Slide and see who has contributed, what has been contributed, and when. It also permits extending the classroom to multiple spaces. Students can be collaborating on a snow day or in the evening and all of us, teacher facilitator included, can be logged on synchronously. The use of digital sources greatly contributes to the success and flexibility of literacy learning clubs as a platform for investigation. Many course management systems from Google Classroom to Canvas to Blackboard to many others offer these types of facilitated experiences in environments that are closed to public inspection, which is often of concern to educators.

Ms. Fischer has spent a significant amount of time helping students understand their role during each component of the literacy learning club, modeling what each step should be like through explicit instruction as well as using the fish bowl technique, a popular collaborative learning structure, where she modeled with other educators a club time session and students observed and commented on what they noticed about the interactions.

In Ms. Fischer's classroom the six groups (four per group) begin their club time with a check-in with one another. Each group member identifies an area he or she is going to pursue. Ms. Fischer has worked with the students to develop a framework for reporting, which includes the following components:

- Locate at least one resource, no more than three during a session.
- Develop a bulleted list of the three core things you learned from the resource.
- Be prepared to share that with the group.

To facilitate this sharing, each group has a shared Google Document that they use to compose notes on their topic. At the conclusion of their individual gathering, the students regroup with their literacy learning club and talk about what they discovered and how that discovery is helping fit into the multimedia template Ms. Fischer developed with each group to share about their position on their topic. This template is made up of four slides that include an overview of the topic, a tagline to persuade the viewer/reader, key research to document, and a final video collage of the position. The students can move back and forth between print and nonprint text as they compose their piece. but they are expected to use a mix of both.

## Focusing Finish

At the conclusion of club time, students should transition from active investigation to reflective synthesis, engaging in the "focusing finish." This helps students organize their time as well as give explicit attention to the value of reflective thinking when securing new learning. This metacognitive conversation may occur face to face or through virtual platforms and can be inclusive of explicit responses to questions such as:

"What did we learn today?"
"How did we come to this new information?"

"What are we still uncertain about?"

"How will we access the information or knowledge still needed?"

This opportunity for reflection helps move students toward the larger goal of developing self-regulated learning as they reflect not only on the content learned but the process they engaged in to support learning. This awareness is helpful in creating the type of independent learner that is guided and sustained by curiosity and not just by classroom expectation. That bridge is essential as we consider our role in supporting 21st-century learning goals and the independence that the CCSS and other standards ask educators to develop.

For those involved in extended club sessions that span multiple meetings, this is also a time to create a blueprint for the next meeting so that students can be formally and informally preparing to convene again. The Appendix offers a variety of examples that can be tailored to suit the area of study.

> In Ms. Fischer's class, the students use this time to review the information gathered as well as the processes used to develop that information. The students know they will be meeting three more times in class for these literacy learning clubs, so they begin organizing their slides for sharing and in doing so identify areas they need to explore further. Google Slides help continue these conversations asynchronously because students can add specific information from home that further bolsters these classroom sessions. Ms. Fischer also appreciates them because they let her easily track contributions.

## Think-Aloud

While students are busy becoming experts on their chosen topic and task, it is also important for the teacher to model expertise as well. The think-aloud offers students the opportunity to see inside the teacher's mind as he or she models and demonstrates the literacy habits of the discipline. It is an opportunity to make our thinking as teachers explicit in a way that helps students understand the literacy steps navigated in a discipline, topic, or text. For example:

- The social scientist may read aloud from a text or think aloud while viewing a video to demonstrate the critical perspective necessary for unpacking historical text.
- The mathematics educator may spend time demonstrating the reading of an equation or word problem, with the focus on the process so that students can learn as well.

- The language arts teacher may read aloud from a genre of study in an effort to model the close reading expectations that allow for success in the literacy learning club at hand.
- The music teacher may model the composition of music in an effort to demonstrate the type of thinking that goes into the composing process.

In many ways, the content of this think-aloud is similar to that of the focusing session described in the beginning of this chapter. Using this opportunity to refocus the class and examine together a specific literacy strategy necessary for success in the club investigation gives students the opportunity to watch and learn with their own experiences in mind. It also provides an opportunity to bring everyone back together in a way that reminds the participants of the learning goals and parameters of the shared work. It is important that this time is specifically linked to the types of literacy experiences students are learning within the content of study in the literacy learning clubs.

> Ms. Fischer gathers the fifth graders back together, informally commenting on the positive work habits she observed as the clubs worked together. Today, since the focus of the literacy learning clubs is print and nonprint persuasive text, Ms. Fischer takes advantage of the political elections to look at ways in which candidates are using persuasive print and nonprint text to engage the viewer. Ms. Fischer models how, when looking at a campaign ad, she notices things like music selected, colors, as well as the content cited, and how together they are meant to persuade her thinking. Ms. Fischer then also models how she can check the accuracy of the information presented, modeling that when a "fact check" demonstrates insincerity, it lessens the text's persuasive value. Ms. Fisher also uses this as an opportunity to model for students the importance of looking deeply into text shared in an effort to make independent decisions.

## Understanding Disciplinary Literacy: Lenses for Learning

In looking at reading across the content areas, we find that there has been a shift from applying universal strategies to specific content to recognizing that the *content* dictates the strategy (Hinchman & Sheridan-Thomas, 2014; Shanahan, 2015). The name change from "content-area reading" to "disciplinary literacy" reflects the belief that each discipline has a unique set of reading and writing skills. Shanahan and colleagues conducted research with disciplinary experts and offered the following findings about the different lenses that readers and writers use (or should be using) when they are engaging with text as a means to understand content. For example, mathematicians are consistently close readers and writers, looking at every word in an attempt to fully understand the content. In Shanahan's study, however, historians were identified as reading for a narrative. Figure 3.2 offers a sample breakdown.

These lenses most often cross paradigms in the ELA class. It is not unusual for ELA to be a place where studying multiple genres happens or where focused study of close reading to fully comprehend dense text occurs. Research suggests, however, that while these skills may be similar to what is needed by disciplinary experts without explicit links offered within the discipline classes themselves, students will not naturally make that connection. Chapters 4 through 8 looks inside the disciplinary literacy practices in the core content areas and the use of the literacy learning clubs paradigm to support learning in these content areas.

## Summary

This chapter explores the literacy learning club paradigm as pieces of a puzzle that fit together to create a pathway for student learning. The pathway explored here is one that is built on the idea that learning is social. Individual acquisition of new knowledge is built on a gradual release of responsibility paradigm that allows understanding to emerge. This is not, however, necessarily a linear transaction but recursive, as explored in Figure 3.1.

In the next several chapters, we take a look inside the core disciplines and consider ways in which this platform may be useful across the disciplines both in traditional self-contained upper elementary grade classrooms and inside the work of content specialists. This framework is applied across disciplines, is flexible

| Discipline | Reading and Writing Lenses |
|---|---|
| English language arts | • To interpret the human experience, often from a specific theoretical lens or position. |
| Social studies | • To contextualize reading and writing within a specific paradigm or point of view.<br>• To work across multiple sources to arrive at a perspective. |
| Science | • To work with multiple texts to locate and present evidence in an attempt to corroborate information. |
| Math | • To work across texts carefully and closely, often rereading multiple times, to identify patterns and key information in an effort to arrive at a truth or answer.<br>• When investigating new, uncorroborated information to read critically to identify possible error. |

**FIGURE 3.2.** What does it mean to read and write? Data from Shanahan (2015).

enough to meet the demands of the curriculum and the students, and is built on the belief that learning is social. The theory and research that support this type of collaborative experience to support adolescent learning will be described and directly connected to the classroom examples in which they are found.

## QUESTIONS FOR REFLECTION

The idea that learning is social extends beyond our discussion of using literacy learning clubs with emerging adolescents and is inclusive of our work with colleagues. As you consider the possibility of implementing this framework into your instruction, there are some questions to consider that are helpful when discussed collaboratively as part of a professional learning community, grade-level conversation, or just informally with a colleague or two. These include:

1. What topics in your discipline might be appropriate for students to investigate as part of a literacy learning club?

2. What learning outcomes do you expect from students at the conclusion of their study of these investigations?

3. What types of artifacts do you anticipate students developing?

4. What types of resources are necessary for students to access?

5. What do students need to be able to do both as readers and writers in order to be successful in this discipline?

6. What potential challenges need to be considered?

## ACTIVITIES TO CONSIDER

Individually or in collaboration, identify a potential area where literacy learning clubs can be integrated into your work. Pilot the implementation. What do you learn? What are you interested in learning more about next time? The remaining chapters offer some insight into this area.

## PART II

# LITERACY LEARNING CLUBS INSIDE THE DISCIPLINES

## CHAPTER 4

# Literacy Learning Clubs
# in English Language Arts

"Wow, I wasn't expecting that."

"Me either, I mean, I thought that they were going to be nicer to Auggie. It made me mad to see those bullies."

"Yes, but it gave Jack a chance to stand up and I think he learned a lot about himself and what is fair and not fair."

"Hmm, yeah, maybe. I don't know. I'm curious what will happen to their friendship after they get back from the trip. Look at this part [points to paragraph and reads silently]. I don't know that makes me think they won't be friends anymore."

This is not a classroom but instead four sixth-grade students who are sitting on the back of a bus and grappling with their reading of *Wonder* by P. J. Palaccio. They chose this book as part of a book club for language arts, but they are so gripped by the content that they talk about it outside of class as well. They are excited, engaged, curious readers thinking about the text as they try and make sense of the content as well as how it relates to their own experience. . . .

This chapter is the first in a series of chapters that looks at the application of literacy learning clubs in the core content disciplines. Literacy learning clubs offer a structure for engaging learners in core content in ways that support the natural development of discipline-specific literacies. In this chapter, I look specifically at how literacy learning clubs offer an avenue for the natural development of the

45

literacy habits necessary for success in ELA in grade 4–8 classrooms. The examples offered are designed to support elementary school teachers who are responsible for multiple subjects as well as those who are content specialists and teach multiple periods of the same subject throughout the day. For the ELA curriculum, it can be an opportunity to take the excitement and enthusiasm engendered by book clubs and connect it to the literacy learning clubs paradigm.

## Disciplinary Literacy: The Literacy Lenses of Readers and Writers

### What Do We Know about Readers and Writers in Grades 4–8?

There is a long-standing myth in literacy education that children's move into fourth grade marks the end of learning to read and the beginning of the time when students start to use *reading to learn,* following through middle school and beyond. There is some truth to this statement. A survey of academic programs in upper elementary grades and middle school classroom documents an expectation, particularly among content specialists, that students have learned the foundations of reading and writing and are ready to access this learning to understand content, investigate literature, and engage as writers (Draper, Broomhead, Jensen, Nokes, & Siebert, 2010; Guthrie, 2015). The CCSS in ELA demand that students read texts of increasing complexity and across digital domains as they move into fourth grade and beyond (Blanchard & Samuels, 2015). The Standards' inclusion of literacy expectations across the disciplines in grades 6–12 signifies the attention the educational community is asked to give to discipline-specific literacy demands (NGO & CCSSO, 2010).

Research on literacy development suggests that there is danger in this assumption that children are reading to learn, particularly in the upper elementary and middle school grades. The belief that literacy foundations are fixed for all learners at age 10 directly correlates to the rise in disengaged readers and writers because the focus shifts from teaching children to teaching texts (Gallagher, 2009; Shanahan, 2015; Tovani, 2011).

Miller and Anderson (2009) describe the kinds of readers we meet in school as developing, dormant, or underground. Miller and Anderson intentionally use descriptors designed to help teachers think differently about the "problem" or "success" cases in the classroom and instead suggest that all readers and writers have needs that educators need to meet. Miller and Anderson suggest many schools are configured to focus on the needs of the developing readers and writers, those who struggle with text. These same schools may offer little incentive for learning for what Miller and Anderson describe as the dormant readers and writers, the students who perform satisfactorily on high-stakes assessment but do not self-identify as readers and writers. They remind educators to pay attention to the underground readers and writers who see the literacy demands of school as disconnected from their own engaged literacy experience as readers and writers happening outside of the school environment (Miller & Anderson, 2009; Miller & Kelley, 2013). Research on literacy engagement supports this claim, observing that while students may continue to engage in literate practice outside of school, their perceptions of the literacy demands during the school day become increasingly negative as they move through the upper grades (Gallagher, 2009; Tovani, 2011). In an era of increased summative assessment and the anxiety educators often feel when these assessments are linked to teacher performance, however misplaced or misunderstood, it is a reasonable finding.

This is a bleak view of literacy learning in the upper elementary and middle school grades. Although some research documents practices that disengage readers and writers, a large body of scholarship documents ELA classrooms (both elementary and middle school) as places where literacy learning is seen as developmental and practices connected to what we know about how adolescents learn are employed (see Alvermann, Fisher, Frey, Kittle, Pearson, Rief, and Tovani, to name just a few). Trends in education suggest that adoption of the CCSS and the increased use of high-stakes assessment are a call to uniform curricula and expectations for children. Using these new adoptions and assessments to standardize curricula and expectations is a misuse and misrepresentation of these trends.

The ILA (formerly the IRA) has made this call to action to educators who work with these students. "Now, more than ever, we need to become active proponents of educational growth—growth that recognizes the importance of high levels of literacy in order for adolescents to achieve their potentials, reach their personal goals, and build a better society" (2012, p. 13). Few would argue with this statement. As educators, we need to consider what advocating for student growth and development involves. Our ELA classrooms are places where students and teachers have the opportunity to use the proven structures and strategies that engage adolescents with text in a way that supports their development and activates their ability to use literacy in its traditional and multimodal forms as the primary vehicle for learning.

Adolescence is a critical developmental juncture, marked by biological, social, and cognitive transformation (Beane & Brodhagen, 2001; Juvonen, Vi-Nhuan, Kaganoff, Augustine, & Constant, 2004). It is surprising that at a time when adolescents are evolving as individuals, many traditional middle school literacy programs attempt to mold students to the curriculum instead of the curriculum to the students (Ivey & Broaddus, 2000; Juvonen et al., 2004; Strauss & Irvin, 2000). A longitudinal study of students' interest in reading from grades 6 through 8 showed a steady decline in both attitude and frequency of independent reading. Results of the study attribute this decline to students' lack of choice and teachers' failure to provide relevant materials (Ley, Schaer, & Dismukes, 1994). There is a strong historical argument, however, that teachers whose literacy programs reflect the unique needs and interests of their students will have more success in educating adolescents (Anders & Pritchard, 1993; Atwell, 2014; Bean, Bean, & Bean, 1999; Biancarosa & Snow, 2004; Dalhouse, Dalhouse, & Mitchell, 1997; IRA, 2012, 2016; Ivey & Fisher, 2007).

The concept of integration is frequently used in research on effective literacy programs throughout the grades. It is "the best of both" approach to instruction; students learn through direct instruction as well as through constructivist or embedded techniques. Accordingly, it is the responsibility of well-informed teachers to use techniques from either "camp" to help students learn. According to this model of literacy instruction, teachers need to offer a wide range of relevant, interesting reading and writing materials that students can use independently as well as provide explicit instruction in comprehension strategies and writing processes (Atwell, 2014; Pressley & Allington, 2015).

## The Growth of Collaboration in Upper Elementary and Middle School ELA Classrooms

Instruction that encourages the social development of adolescents has proven effective as well. When adolescents work in small groups with their peers, they are more likely to take risks and literacy improves. Adolescents who have the opportunity to work and learn with their peers in partnerships and small-group collaborations tend to be more successful because they are more engaged (Almasi & Garas-York, 2009; Guthrie, 2015; Harvey & Daniels, 2015).

My interest in literacy learning clubs grew from my own observation as a classroom teacher of how engaged youth and adolescent readers and writers become during book clubs (Daniels, 2002). When I first started teaching middle school, I had the opportunity to attend a workshop series hosted by Harvey Daniels, and I was immediately inspired. Since then, my teaching and research have been guided by the principle that collaborative learning experiences have a deeper influence on individual learning than when working in isolation. What inspired me as a novice teacher and continues to excite my interest in and curiosity about children's and adolescent's learning is the unscripted nature of this approach and its foundation in professional beliefs about teaching and learning. This framework and those that have evolved since, as well as the literacy learning clubs described throughout this book, rely on the educator's professionalism to adopt and adapt based on the unique contexts in which he or she is situated. This is not a scripted curriculum but a pedagogical choice that is informed by research and theory and relies on the professional expertise of the educators involved to integrate in ways that are supportive of the students she or he teaches.

There have been many adoptions and iterations of book clubs in ELA classrooms. Harvey Daniels changed the term from "literature circles" to "book clubs" to reflect the shifting texts that are at the center of these social collaborations. Most recently, he and his colleague Stephanie Harvey have moved this work further to take a look inside inquiry circles where questions motivate the investigation of texts (2015).

How am I conceptualizing book clubs? Essentially, these are small groups formed around students' interest in identified texts. This concept began as literature circles where classroom teachers offered a menu of fictional texts to students and assigned specific roles to readers in an effort to make explicit the work that engaged readers use naturally (Daniels, 2002). This carefully scaffolded experience was designed around the gradual release of responsibility model (Pearson & Gallagher, 1983), with the explicit anchors or roles being pulled away as these students in grades 4–8 began to naturally adopt the role of readers in a book club. Concern that role sheets were being used as scripted worksheets has led to explicit conversations around creating book clubs as places where organic and natural conversations around reading occur with scaffolding, as necessary by the expert (teacher) in the room.

This practice is a staple in many ELA classrooms. In a well-balanced program, it is one avenue through which literacy development is encouraged. This is true for both self-contained elementary classrooms and the departmentalized middle school model. The need to engage developing adolescents is critical, and book clubs offer one opportunity to support these students by engaging them in an academic setting in the very social worlds that are developmentally significant for them. It integrates well in the ELA classroom, which is often the place where these small-group collaborations work and where learning strategies to dive deeply into text is generally an essential part of the curriculum. This is, however, just one piece of the learning puzzle. In an effective literacy program, opportunity for whole-group investigations as well as individual study of reading and writing must also be part of the program if we are going to positively and effectively support the literacy development of adolescents.

## *What Can We Learn from Book Clubs?*

Book clubs have had an impact on ELA classrooms as they become places where social interaction is encouraged. In these small groups, students argue, appreciate, and *engage* in literature, and it is the collaborative structure that offers the pathway for more engaged and therefor more productive learning. Some argue that this is not the instructional part of the day, and in some ways that is true. It is only a piece of the program, but I suggest it is the piece where students develop their identities as readers and writers through relationships and build ownership of the skills and strategies that are being taught in other places during the literacy block.

The fourth-grade literacy slump, then, is it real? The answer is yes and no. As educators, we have to be cautious not to enact practices grounded in myth. Instead, we need to carefully align practices that can be documented by research (ILA, 2016; Pressley & Allington, 2015). There is evidence that students in the upper elementary grades become less responsive to school-based literacy demands (Gallagher, 2009; IRA, 2012). This disinterest may correlate, however, with the academic shift that places core content rather than the learner at the center of learning. Classrooms then become less differentiated and less focused on the developmental needs of the students in the room and more on the curricular and standards benchmarks. Research on best practices in language arts/literacy document that it is not an either/or question but a balance of both (Pressley & Allington, 2015).

What if we were to continue to teach the learner as a pathway to the learning? What if we privileged both? That is the rationale behind literacy learning clubs in all classrooms, but it is perhaps easiest to integrate in the ELA classroom that is already positioned to focus on literacy demands and often embraces book clubs. In Chapters 5–8, we look inside the core content disciplines that are not typically positioned for this type of learning and describe ways in which literacy learning clubs can become a platform for supporting students' understanding of the discipline and specific core content.

A range of literature is available that engages fourth through eighth graders. Schools are slow to change, but the surge in well-written, engaging young adult literature offers a menu through which school-based literacy becomes a pathway for engaged learning. Consider the U.S. ambassador for young adult literature that began with Kate DiCamello and has recently been awarded to a graphic novelist and former teacher, Gene Yang. I recently surveyed a group of novice middle school language arts teachers about what creates a "canon," a term used frequently by English educators to identify core pieces of literature; together we identified the importance of enduring themes such as love, family, and tragedy, and then we highlighted recent young adult texts that offered the opportunity to investigate these themes in a context through which emerging adolescents could readily find connection. This becomes the place to begin.

In addition, as we have explored in the previous chapters, the new literacies that students navigate as a vehicle for social collaboration and connection are resources for implementing this framework for academic use. The growing trend in upper elementary and middle school classrooms whereby electronic devices are supplied and students are equipped with digital tools much in the way they used to be assigned textbooks marks a recent and rapid shift that is transforming the way classroom space is understood. Recently, I taught a course to practicing teachers that was delivered through synchronous and asynchronous sessions. Students never came to campus, but we met together frequently using a synchronous virtual platform in which we interacted just as we might if we were sitting in the same room. Our classroom space was defined by the virtual community we created, and it did not exist in bricks and mortar.

In one of the fourth-grade classrooms I work in regularly, the students have created a "tweeter" role as part of their regular book club meetings, and the person in that role tweets out about their conversation. In some classes, there is a live Twitter account, and in others it is simulated. In another classroom across the hall, book clubs are operating jointly, with a teacher in Michigan found through the Global Reads program. Social media have become a way for all readers to engage in the social practice of book clubs without sitting side by side. The hashtag (#) has organized learning in ways that are transformative as the community exists within the virtual thread and not a fixed room. As we examined in Chapter 3 and will thread through the examples shared here and in subsequent chapters, the digital world is shifting our sense of classroom space and community in ways that we are only just beginning to understand.

## Literacy Learning Clubs in ELA Classrooms

Literacy learning clubs in the ELA classroom have *topic* at their center instead of *text*. There is demonstrated success in collaborative work around subjects that capitalize on theme-based investigations (Harvey & Daniels, 2015). In the ELA classroom, literacy learning clubs become a place where a topic or theme and not the text drives the conversation, and the texts are drawn in as needed to support the shared investigation.

What might this look like in an ELA classroom? It might include a study (selected from a menu of options) of representations of the community in fourth grade, and the texts become maps, short stories, and nonfiction accounts of the state in which the children live. In an eighth-grade classroom, it becomes a place where students are studying genres and select from a menu of options to learn more about the characteristics of specific genres. As we step inside the classrooms of Ms. L and Mr. R, we see this come alive.

What needs to be in place before beginning? First, as teachers we need to develop relationships with our students and have them develop professional relationships with one another (Garrett, 2014). In the English classroom, it is helpful if book clubs have already been in place because then students are already comfortable with the social exchanges that are part of the learning as well as the individual accountability necessary for group success (Casey, 2012a, 2012b).

Next, we need to consider the curriculum and standards that are aligned with the grade level and ask what units of study invite literacy learning clubs as a pathway for learning. For example, in Ms. Fischer's fifth-grade classroom that we peeked inside in Chapter 3, groups were formed based on the topic the students were most interested in investigating from the options provided. Then, persuasive text was studied as a way to articulate the position the individual group members and/or the group as a whole was taking on the topic. This same approach can be taken across the grade levels with topics appropriate to the grade level, curriculum, and context of the classroom. The literacy learning club model supports the current move to increase exposure to multiple genres and formats because thematic study motivates students to survey a wide range of print and nonprint materials (Blanchard & Samuels, 2015; Casey et al., 2014; CCSS, 2010).

Time allotted for ELA always needs to be considered. Generally, self-contained elementary classrooms feel a bit more flexible because they are not bound by the bell. Even that has shifted, however, as some schools and districts impose strict guidelines on time spent on content, as shifts in standards and assessment dictate pressure all along the educational continuum. Generally, 40 minutes of time is ideal to allow students to move through the literacy learning club meeting cycle. The number of meetings around a topic is dependent on the topic of study. This, too, is a place where degree of flexibility is dependent on the context. In some instances, teachers are bound to be at particular places in the curriculum by specific dates, which creates a strict timeline for group meetings. In others, the ability to observe how the group is moving forward and extends or retracts time allows for a responsiveness that is ideal but not always practical in all settings.

Recent trends in ELA pedagogy include the infusion of increasingly complex texts and an increase in attention to nonfiction. In states that have adopted the CCSS, it is expected that by grades 9–12, 70% of what students read will be nonfiction. Many ELA teachers invite this paradigm by blending fiction and nonfiction texts around thematic or topical areas of study. Literacy learning clubs invite an opportunity to naturally connect what had previously been taught as disparate genres because they are organized around a topic and not a text type.

## Literacy Learning Clubs in Practice: Voices from the Classroom

### Ms. L's Fourth-Grade Classroom

Ms. L is in her fourth year of teaching fourth grade in a culturally diverse community. The 22 children in her classroom reflect the middle/high SES (socioeconomic status) of the community in which she teaches, and there is a large degree of parental involvement. "Too much" Ms. L will sometimes lovingly say as she works diligently to ensure that she is incorporating the wealth of parent volunteers into the classroom in a way that is productive for student learning.

Ms. L has found success, particularly in the area of student engagement, with book clubs since she began teaching. It is an established part of the curriculum, and for the most part students come to Ms. L having experienced book clubs in their language arts classrooms in the past. This year, Ms. L is implementing literacy learning clubs after her students have completed a book club. Ms. L began with "what they knew" (i.e., book clubs) so that they could use the small-group framework to integrate topic instead of text.

Ms. L's students' last book club focused on understanding difference, and to that end students enjoyed productive conversations around the texts *Fish in a Tree* (Hunt, 2011), *Wonder* (Palacio, 2012), *Out of My Mind* (Draper, 2010), and *Rules* (Lord, 2000). At the conclusion of their book clubs, they created book trailers, which led to a class conversation about the various types of "difference" they explored through the lens of the fictional characters. These differences included dyslexia (*Fish in a Tree*), rare disfigurement (*Wonder*), cerebral palsy (*Out of My Mind*), and autism (*Rules*). When the class wanted to understand more, Ms. L proposed the use of literacy learning clubs as a vehicle for exploring these topics.

They began by identifying the topic they were most interested in becoming more expert on, which may or may not have related to the text in which it was connected. Next, Ms. L formed groups, and the class established a time line. They agreed on 3 weeks, with two meetings per week and decided to do a digital poster session (*www.smore.com*) at the end to share their learning with each other, the school community, and parents. These students had easy and comfortable access to technology and the Internet outside of school, and frequently small-group conversations that began in class spilled over to asynchronous contributions outside of class.

The class launched their literacy learning club investigation with Ms. L offering a mini-lesson on strategies for conducting online searches for topics. Ms. L, along with the media center specialist, provided support during that initial meeting to model how to refine searches and how to be cautious with unknown sites. For example, Ms. L modeled for the students the difference between reading a parent's blog about having a child with autism and reading a study about the disorder. These were two examples of nonfiction but two very different text types within that broad category. This was used as an opportunity to talk about reading material with a critical lens. Ms. L learned that her fourth graders often assumed that anything that seemed to resemble nonfiction offered objective facts, and considering personal blogs in comparison to research studies provided an opportunity to discuss the different goals and perspectives of the author and the nuances that make the two nonfiction text types different.

The class then went into their club meeting that Ms. L had scheduled for 30 minutes during the 90-minute language arts block the class had on Tuesdays and Thursdays. The class met for six sessions, and while Ms. L always saw the need for the time to continue, she balanced that with the demands of the curriculum and the other supports necessary for student learning.

Ms. L is fortunate to have a large number of parents who are available and interested in volunteering during the school day. Prior to beginning the book clubs, she invites parents who are interested in being facilitators during these sessions to come in for a conversation about the approach and the goals for the students. Ms. L conducts a 30-minute training session for parent volunteers on how to use questions to encourage independent thinking in students and details the types of resources available for students.

For 3 weeks the groups meet. Each meeting begins with Ms. L directing students' attention to a literacy strategy to support their research of their chosen area. The students then gather to identify goals for the session, and each member takes a role in completing those goals. For example, in session three, Ms. L launches a focusing lesson on how to create questions to talk with people who have in some way experienced first hand any of these challenges that they are investigating. After modeling methods for creating and asking effective questions, the students in each group begin to work together to develop questions they are interested in learning more about. Then the group decides who will be responsible for interviewing different people that they have identified as interested in talking about their topic. The students essentially "assign" each other the tasks, and then they establish the time line for completion. This is Thursday, and given the limited number of meetings left, each student agrees to tape and write up the 5-minute interview to share with one another via Google Docs and then to assimilate into their shared presentation the following week. While the group only has 40 minutes of dedicated classroom time, the use of Google Documents and Google Hangouts gives the students the opportunity to continue collaborating synchronously and asynchronously as needed.

At the conclusion of this session of learning clubs, the students create a virtual poster session using Smore, an online service for developing interactive online posters that is initially available to the class members for comment and then shared with the parents and the wider school community. At the conclusion of the experience, all of the students feel empowered and more informed about the challenges that drew them in as readers of fiction during their book club session.

At each phase, students are actively engaged in the necessary literacy skills that are benchmarked by the CCSS. This is also true as the students develop academic writing and vocabulary. This natural inquiry is not in spite of the Standards but directly touches on the skills required. For example, these students have had the opportunity to:

CCSS.ELA-LITERACY.RI.4.3: Explain events, procedures, ideas, or concepts in a historical, scientific, or technical text, including what happened and why, based on specific information in the text.

CCSS.ELA-LITERACY.RI.4.9: Integrate information from two texts on the same topic in order to write or speak about the subject knowledgeably.

CCSS.ELA-LITERACY.RI.4.7: Interpret information presented visually, orally, or quantitatively (e.g., in charts, graphs, diagrams, time lines, animations, or interactive elements on web pages) and explain how the information contributes to an understanding of the text in which it appears.

CCSS.ELA-LITERACY.W.4.2: Write informative/explanatory texts to examine a topic and convey ideas and information clearly. (NGA & CCSSO, 2010)

Ultimately, the students are driven by "the need to know," and the teacher serves to facilitate/guide and name the literacy skills and strategies needed to acquire the information. It is a shift. The students start with the real-world question, and then the teacher helps name the specific standards, skills, and strategies students are using so that they become aware of how accessing these core literacy skills are necessary not simply for school success, but for life success. For example, in order to better understand some of the conditions Ms. L models how she reads across different sources, including websites and information found in printed text. She notes how the source matters and that before she identifies something as a fact, particularly when found on the internet, she looks for confirmation elsewhere. Throughout, the students are deeply engaged in reading and writing both print and nonprint materials.

## Mr. S's Eighth-Grade Classroom

Mr. S has been teaching eighth-grade language arts for 2 years. In the urban middle school where Mr. S teaches, the students have eight 45-minute blocks (periods), one of which is ELA. Mr. S sees five different sections of students, all heterogeneously grouped, throughout the school day. Prior to coming to middle school, Mr. S was a high school English teacher where he primarily used whole-class novels as directed by the curriculum. Mr. S has been engaged deeply with professional reading and is shifting from teaching text to teaching children. Mr. S was recently introduced to the use of book clubs by a colleague and has found them to be a compelling method for engaging the adolescent readers and writers in his classroom.

The school where Mr. S teaches is composed of a diverse group of students who represent a range of economic and linguistic backgrounds. Mr. S loves the diversity but is challenged by traditional notions of the whole-class approach to English education. Mr. S has turned to literacy learning clubs as a way to engage his eighth-grade students as well as accommodate the continuum of literacy skills in his classroom. This school has been identified as "in need of improvement" because of students' poor performance on the high-stakes assessments, so he feels pressure to help his students' scores improve. Mr. S is getting some pushback from colleagues about using book clubs and now literacy learning clubs in the classroom because they require time and they limit the direct instruction and focused test preparation that many of the students in the other classrooms are engaging in daily.

## Learning Clubs as a Pathway for Supporting a Study of Writing

Mr. S wants to be responsive to what he is coming to believe is a preferred practice while also maintaining the school culture's drive toward improving academic performance both locally in the classroom and in relation to national assessments. He decides to balance this by launching into his first literacy learning clubs with an investigation of the forms of writing that are required by the CCSS as *Text Types and Purposes*. The eighth-grade CCSS require the following:

CCSS.ELA-LITERACY.W.8.1: Write arguments to support claims with clear reasons and relevant evidence.

CCSS.ELA-LITERACY.W.8.2: Write informative/explanatory texts to examine a topic and convey ideas, concepts, and information through the selection, organization, and analysis of relevant content.

CCSS.ELA-LITERACY.W.8.3: Write narratives to develop real or imagined experiences or events using effective technique, relevant descriptive details, and well-structured event sequences. (NGA & CCSSO, 2010).

Mr. S, fresh off the success of book clubs, decides to maintain the collaborative conversations in a study of writing genres in an effort to improve students' understanding of the different text types and approaches they need to take as writers.

Mr. S begins by engaging the class in a school issue that has been dominating the students' concerns. Due to the low assessment scores, the school board is looking into extending the school day to allow for more time for study in an effort to improve performance. The students and faculty have a range of opinions about this possibility, and at the heart of the topics is the question: "Is there a relationship between time spent in school and performance on high-stakes assessments?" This question provokes a range of conversations, including quality not quantity, the value of co-curricular participation, and the need for more time for advanced study of complex texts. Mr. S suggests that it is through writing that these ideas can be better explored and shared with others and that in doing so it is necessary to look at how the different text types convey information.

Mr. S then creates a menu of subtopics from the large question of study that is inclusive of some of the items above such as the value of co-curricular participation, the link between time in school and success on high-stakes assessment, and the organization of time to reflect quality instructions. These topics come out of a class conversation that is held virtually through *www.padlet.com* and then brought to class for continued oral discussion. Mr. S reflects that this menu is one that educators themselves could explore as they identify their own positions on this "hot topic."

Groups are formed based on area of interest, and then Mr. S engages in a series of mini-lessons on text types both as readers and writers. The groups locate digital texts that reflect narrative, informational, and argument around their identified subtopics and use their developing understanding of the genre as a reader to better understand point of view and tools of persuasion. Newsela (*www.newsela.com*) is a popular source, as are Scholastic for Kids (*www.scholasticforkids.com*) and various periodicals. This critical reading of the texts leads to each group developing a focused understanding of their topic. The groups themselves then create these text types, describing their topic in an effort to share perspectives and inform understanding. The class works for 3 weeks in their groups during their 40-minute sessions. Generally, Mr. S begins each class with a mini-lesson on how to understand a specific text type as well as how to link these to digital reading/writing experiences. The groups then work collaboratively to identify individual roles during each session of researching and note taking. Much of their individual work is done on a shared Google Doc to allow for collaboration. Mr. S is known to frequently offer his own perspectives/ideas/questions in these spaces in an effort to elevate and guide the discussions. Each student in each group is responsible for developing a piece that is reflective of each text type studied, which for this investigation is both memoir and expository text. Together with their group, they conference and edit one another's work. While the focus is on the printed word, the students are encouraged to link to nonprint resources as well to share the information studied.

These resources are collected and shared on Google Docs as the class develops an edited volume titled *School Time: What We Make of Every Minute*, with a chapter for each topic. Mr. S retains the role of executive editor as he works with each group to move their individual pieces to final copy. In doing so, the class is engaged in the topic that is creating a lot of stir in the building, and the necessary academic writing becomes the tool to explore the relevant issue. Just as in Ms. L's classroom, the question drives the learning, and the explicit instruction around the necessary text types that are part of the CCSS is brought in to support this authentic investigation. This digital volume is then shared with the school community for comment and conversation.

## Summary

ELA classrooms are places where book clubs are often integrated into the curriculum to support and engage readers. This creates a natural pathway for integrating literacy learning clubs into these classrooms because there is an understanding of the value of social collaboration to support reading and writing development. The key difference is that a focused theme or question now drives the club instead of a core text. It is a natural integration and a useful place to begin for schools considering adopting literacy learning clubs into the program.

## QUESTIONS FOR REFLECTION

1. In looking at the curriculum with which you work, where are places that literacy learning clubs may support and engage the students in your classroom?

2. Consider the case studies. What reactions, questions, and comments do you have to the work of these teachers? How can we learn from them and extend their work for our students?

3. What role can literacy learning clubs play in supporting literacy learning? Where do they fit within an overall ELA program?

## ACTIVITIES TO CONSIDER

- Design a literacy learning club framework for an upcoming curricular topic in ELA. Consider the Appendix as a resource for developing the plan.

- Survey your students about their literacy habits inside and outside of school (see the sample survey in the Appendix). This may be a helpful tool for designing instruction around the literacy needs of the students with whom you work.

## CHAPTER 5

# Literacy Learning Clubs in Social Studies

Heads are clustered around a computer screen. Students are eagerly scrolling through photographs that were recently discovered in the basement of a school library and scanned into the town's digital archives. It shows children sitting in a room that is remarkably unchanged from the one these children find themselves in wearing very different clothing and holding different types of books. Questions are being thrown out around the table:

"I wonder when this is?"

"Can you see the title of the book? Let's see if we can find the publication date."

"Probably the same math book we are using now [children laugh]."

The children continue to investigate, digging deeper, noticing differences across race and gender roles, using their 21st-century resources to enter the 20th-century world that seems right at their fingertips and yet is over a century away. In this moment they are historians, working with primary source documents against secondary pieces of information to craft a narrative that describes the life experience of these students nearly 100 years ago. . . .

Social studies instruction is inclusive of a broad range of disciplines. The National Council for the Social Studies (NCSS, n.d.) offers this description:

NCSS defines social studies as "the integrated study of the social sciences and humanities to promote civic competence." Within the school program, social studies provides coordinated, systematic study drawing upon such disciplines as anthropology, archaeology, economics, geography, history, law, philosophy, political science, psychology, religion, and sociology, as well as appropriate content from the humanities, mathematics, and natural sciences. In essence, social studies promotes knowledge of and involvement in civic affairs. And because civic issues—such as health care, crime, and foreign policy—are multidisciplinary in nature, understanding these issues and developing resolutions to them require multidisciplinary education. These characteristics are the key defining aspects of social studies.

To this end, the NCSS advocates for considering curriculum thematically through the lens of these 10 themes:

1. Culture.
2. Time, continuity, and change.
3. People, places, and environments.
4. Individual development and identity.
5. Individuals, groups, and institutions.
6. Power, authority, and governance.
7. Production, distribution, and consumption.
8. Science, technology, and society.
9. Global connections.
10. Civic ideals and practices.

Currently, states develop their own set of standards around the framework established by the NCSS, and many social studies educators describe the arduous task of deciding what content should be included or excluded within a set of standards and curriculum. Looking through the lens of themes and then applying to these thematic studies the various disciplines within social studies offers the comprehensive avenue into student learning that the NCSS recommends. This perspective aligns with the paradigm of literacy learning clubs presented in this text, which suggests that collaborative experiences around a shared topic motivate natural inquiry and the purposeful use of discipline specific literacy to learn.

In this chapter, I step inside literacy learning clubs as a tool for learning in a social studies classroom. Literacy learning clubs offer a structure for engaging learners in core social studies content in ways that support the natural development of discipline-specific literacies and reject traditional paradigms of students as passive recipients of facts and features of a discipline. Here I look specifically at how literacy learning clubs allow the natural development of the literacy habits necessary for success in understanding social studies content in grade 4–8 class-rooms. The examples offered are designed to support elementary school teachers who are responsible for multiple subjects as well as those who are content special-ists and teach multiple periods of social studies throughout the day and any range of approaches along this continuum.

Social studies is inclusive of diverse content, so while you are reading this chapter and stepping inside the classrooms within the "Voices from the Class-room" section, it is useful to consider strategies for adapting this framework to the particular social studies curriculum you are considering using the literacy learning club paradigm to investigate. Many of the examples offered in this chapter enter social studies through the lens of history and political science, not as a surface study of dates and events but as an umbrella through which these core themes recommended by the NCSS can be understood.

Study of the political and cultural structures of ancient China, for example, gives students the opportunity to develop the capacity to analyze how societal structures influence individuals. Developing this cognitive framework allows stu-dents to begin to develop the capacity to analyze the current structures surround-ing their own environment. Content learning and conceptual understanding are developing because of one another. Using themes alongside skills or specific time periods, people, or places invites an integrated use of the various areas of social studies outlined by the NCSS.

## Disciplinary Literacy: The Literacy Lenses of Social Scientists

In a study of the literacy habits of disciplinary experts, Shanahan, Shanahan, and Misischia (2011) surveyed historians to determine the literacy skills needed for success in their work. Their findings suggest that historians recognize the need to use multiple text types that include primary and secondary sources when examin-ing moments in history. To effectively access this content, students need a strong understanding of the various text structures and features they are reading and writing.

These social scientists were attuned to the relationship between narrative and argument. Historians believe that, in order to arrive at an understanding of a spe-cific time period or event, texts need to be read in relation to one another because this will allow the reader to evaluate and ultimately develop a comprehensive understanding of the time period, topic, or theme. Similarly, as writers, historians draw on these sources to create their own historical narrative and argument; in doing so, they are acutely aware that their own positions need to be documented as they influence their findings. Shanahan et al. (2011) offer the following in their findings:

> These historians, during the focus group discussions, expressed abhorrence at the idea of instruction including only a single textbook in a high school history class because sourcing and corroboration are so central to history reading, and neither would be possible with only a single text. It was not that they were opposed to the idea of using a textbook for such classes, but only that such a textbook would have to be supplemented with other primary and secondary sources if students were to be afforded the opportunity to engage in authentic history reading. (p. 423)

So what does that look like in practice? It begins not with the text or the facts, but instead with the question or theme as outlined by the NCSS. Then multiple text types that are inclusive of specific facts are drawn together in order to understand the "big idea" (Draper, 2010; Duke, 2014; Nokes, 2010).

When learning about World War II, for example, students as young as fourth grade may read *The Diary of Ann Frank*, a narrative, alongside maps and figures of the patterns of battle, textbook analysis, and summary of the events, as well as video footage and still photographs. To get at content, students need to be able to understand how the text type they are working with positions meaning (i.e., author's argument, source, perspective). In addition, there is the implicit expectation that students will synthesize knowledge gained through these various text types to arrive at their own general understanding of the topic or theme, World War II. This is a sophisticated series of literacy moves, and in content-focused classes the danger is that we may not be offering students enough information about the text structure itself and the literacy strategies needed to work within these text types, so students are left to discover how to negotiate these moves on their own.

Shanahan (2015) took this research and mapped it on to social studies pedagogy and suggests that in social studies students must "read multiple genres, understand the language of history, and write history" (p. 12). Shanahan et al. (2011) also analyzed the discourse patterns of historians and noted that when engaging as readers and writers in social studies, understanding the discipline-specific genres is necessary:

> Coffin (1997) classified common genres of history to include (a) historical recount (to retell the events in a sequence), (b) historical account (to account for why things happened in a particular sequence), (c) historical explanation (to explain past events by examining cause and effect), and (d) historical argument (to advocate a particular interpretation). (p. 398)

This paradigm will help students analyze text structure as well as structure texts themselves.

This view of what it means to read and write like a social scientist recognizes the importance of disciplinary literacy. This is a departure from content-area literacy, which suggests that generalizable literacy skills and strategies can be mapped on to all disciplines. Instead, looking at content from a disciplinary literacy lens suggests that there are distinct patterns of what it means to successfully read and write within each discipline, and it is through those patterns that we enter instruction. We continue to explore this phenomenon in the next several chapters, which look inside mathematics and science. Understanding content-area reading and writing as *disciplinary literacy*, the unique literacy skills necessary for success within the discipline being studied, is at the heart of literacy learning clubs in social studies classes as well as in the other disciplines explored in this book (Draper, 2010; Duke, 2014; Fisher & Frey, 2015; Shanahan, 2015). Similarly, the CCSS recognize these unique skills within the standards in their call to infuse discipline-specific literacy instruction within the core content areas (see the *Common Core State Standards in Grades 6–12 Literacy in History/Social Studies, Science, & Technical Subjects*, available at *www.corestandards.org/ELA-Literacy/RH/introduction*).

## Literacy Learning Clubs in Social Studies Classrooms

### Literacy Learning Clubs in Elementary Social Studies Classrooms

Social studies is often cited as the discipline that receives the least amount of instructional time in the elementary grades. The 2010 National Assessment of Educational Programs (NAEP) data confirm this claim, noting that 80% of fourth-grade students had teachers who reported spending approximately 61 minutes per week on social studies. This number jumps to 95% of teachers spending 3 or more hours in eighth grade (see Figures 5.1 and 5.2).

This time spent on social studies learning in the elementary grades has continued to diminish as high-stakes assessments in language arts and math have increased (Fitchett, Heafner, & Van Fossen, 2014). Fitchett et al. (2014) found that when social studies is integrated into the ELA, more time is devoted to the content. They note:

> Moreover, results indicate that integration of social studies content into ELA instruction is positively associated with increased time for social studies and more frequent dynamic instruction. We encourage teacher-leaders to collaborate

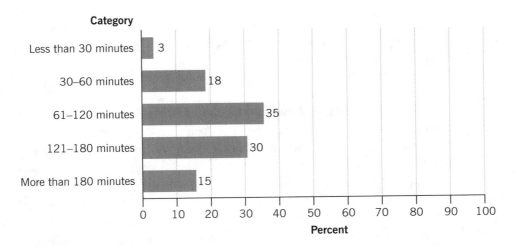

**FIGURE 5.1.** Classroom context: Time spent on social studies (fourth grade). As part of the 2010 NAEP civics assessment, teachers of fourth and eighth graders were asked, "About how much time in total do you spend with your class on social studies instruction in a typical week?" Possible responses were less than 30 minutes, 30 to 60 minutes, 61 to 120 minutes, 121 to 180 minutes, and more than 180 minutes. About 80% of fourth-grade students had teachers who reported spending 61 minutes or more on social studies instruction in a typical week. From NAEP (2010).

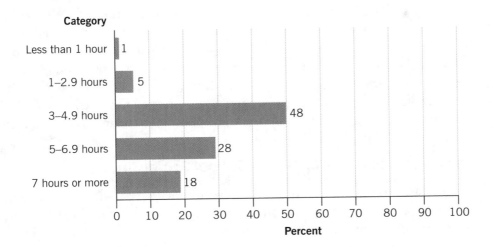

**FIGURE 5.2.** Classroom context: Time spent on social studies (eighth grade). As part of the 2010 civics assessment, teachers of fourth and eighth graders were asked, "About how much time in total do you spend with your class on social studies instruction in a typical week?" Possible responses were less than 1 hour, 1–2.9 hours, 3–4.9 hours, 5–6.9 hours, and 7 hours or more. About 95% of eighth-grade students had teachers who reported spending 3 hours or more on social studies instruction in a typical week. From NAEP (2010).

and share ideas for using integration as an effective strategy for improving over-all social studies instruction among grade levels. Finding curricular spaces in which social studies can share instructional time with other subjects, specifi-cally ELA, is a practical step toward improving overall instruction. (p. 25)

These findings make sense. In many elementary classrooms, instruction in math and language arts frequently spill into the "time" reserved for social studies; as a result, time spent engaging in social studies learning is minimal. In addition, it is common practice in elementary classrooms to cycle between science and social studies. This flawed practice often begins in the preservice years when minimal time is spent on methods instruction in both science and social studies pedagogy; this sends the message that these content areas have limited value (Fitchett et al., 2014). In my own institution, we currently offer a blended-methods 3-credit-hour-course, Teaching Science, Social Studies and the Arts, to our K–6 certification candidates, while Teaching Math is its own 3-credit-hour course and Teaching Literacy is two 3-credit-hour courses. It is not enough to say that the disciplines of social studies and science are embedded within language arts and math.

Research linking disciplinary literacy and work advocated for by the NCSS suggests that the solution is more than simply infusing social studies texts into the language arts instructional period in the upper elementary self-contained class-room. Instead, we need to go beyond integration toward transformative study that allows students as young as fourth grade (and perhaps even earlier) as well as mid-dle school students to recognize the different lenses they use to access social stud-ies content. The literacy learning clubs paradigm that puts topic instead of text at the center of collaborative investigations suggests that students acquire social studies content when they learn the specific literacy skills needed to navigate the information providing them with tools that are not limited to the classroom. We explore this point in our "Voices from the Classroom" section later in the chapter.

## Literacy Learning Clubs in Middle School Social Studies

A dramatic shift in time spent on social studies instruction occurs when students enter middle school. There is a range of content that students and teachers are expected to work with in these grades. Suddenly, students who may have had very little experience with social studies, taught by teachers who may have had insuf-ficient preparation in the methods of social studies instruction, are expected to demonstrate expertise. It is no surprise that many of these students struggle as they make this leap. Social studies in the middle school typically receives similar time as the other content areas, and students suddenly find themselves working with disciplinary experts who may have limited understanding of the literacy demands needed to negotiate the content.

The CSSS in ELA offer specific criteria for middle school instruction defined by the standards as grades 6–8 in history/social studies. As readers and writers of the discipline, students are expected to engage in the following in social studies:

### Key Ideas and Details

CCSS.ELA-LITERACY.RH.6-8.1: Cite specific textual evidence to support analysis of primary and secondary sources.

CCSS.ELA-LITERACY.RH.6-8.2: Determine the central ideas or information of a primary or secondary source; provide an accurate summary of the source distinct from prior knowledge or opinions.

CCSS.ELA-LITERACY.RH.6-8.3: Identify key steps in a text's description of a process related to history/social studies (e.g., how a bill becomes law, how interest rates are raised or lowered).

### Craft and Structure

CCSS.ELA-LITERACY.RH.6-8.4: Determine the meaning of words and phrases as they are used in a text, including vocabulary specific to domains related to history/social studies.

CCSS.ELA-LITERACY.RH.6-8.5: Describe how a text presents information (e.g., sequentially, comparatively, causally).

CCSS.ELA-LITERACY.RH.6-8.6: Identify aspects of a text that reveal an author's point of view or purpose (e.g., loaded language, inclusion or avoidance of particular facts).

### Integration of Knowledge and Ideas

CCSS.ELA-LITERACY.RH.6-8.7: Integrate visual information (e.g., in charts, graphs, photographs, videos, or maps) with other information in print and digital texts.

CCSS.ELA-LITERACY.RH.6-8.8: Distinguish among fact, opinion, and reasoned judgment in a text.

CCSS.ELA-LITERACY.RH.6-8.9: Analyze the relationship between a primary and secondary source on the same topic.

### Range of Reading and Level of Text Complexity

CCSS.ELA-LITERACY.RH.6-8.10: By the end of grade 8, read and comprehend history/social studies texts in the grades 6–8 text complexity band independently and proficiently. (NGA & CCSSO, 2010)

These skills refer to the discipline-specific habits necessary for success in the social sciences. (Nokes, 2010; Shanahan et al., 2011; Shanahan, 2015). Essentially, students of the discipline must be able to move across the various text types specific to the social sciences that include reading multiple sources (i.e., primary and secondary sources—oral, visual, and written) centered on the same topic. This is a sophisticated type of reading that requires understanding different text structures, reading for both content as well as the underlying motive of the author, and linking these together to arrive at meaning.

The availability of many primary sources digitally offers the opportunity to broaden traditional conceptions of textbook-driven social studies instruction. Textbook-driven instruction is ineffective in both engaging students in the content and building the skills necessary for fully understanding the discipline in ways that allows students to apply the skills outside of the classroom (Fitchett et al., 2014). The rise of virtual field trips, the accessibility of virtual reality with accessible simple-to-use devices (e.g., Google cardboard), along with the digitization of many primary source documents and collections, means that studying these documents and places is often only a point and a click away. The need to read and write a variety of text types when learning social studies demonstrates the necessity to begin building these skills in the elementary grades so that students become increasingly comfortable weaving sources together to arrive at meaning and then putting together their findings using the same multiple modes of text that they negotiated when investigating the topic.

Think about the last United States election cycle. Arriving at an individual perspective required a careful sifting of information across still and moving images and spoken and printed texts, with a careful eye to the source of the information. The ability to consider text source and structure alongside the content presented is crucial for full comprehension to occur. This "life-readiness" skill must begin in the elementary grades and continue into middle school and high school, with explicit attention given to the strategies effective readers and writers adopt when working across multiple text types to comprehend and construct meaning. Literacy learning clubs offer a framework that helps students develop these skills.

For example, studying the civil rights movement involves more than simply reading a chapter in a textbook. It is possible to view original footage of demonstrations, to hear accounts from those in attendance representing a variety of positions, and to read the actual newspaper articles written at the time through public access to digital archives. Such a project requires helping students understand *how* to read these different text types with the healthy skepticism needed as well as demonstrating *where* to find the information. Working across multiple print and nonprint resources is a sophisticated literacy task that requires careful study of the form of each to weave together meaning.

The literacy learning club paradigm offers an opportunity to build these skills through authentic study because at the heart of the investigation is the chance to seek out information in ways that naturally motivate the participants to draw on these multiple resources and to arrive at their own answers. The same skills that are described in the CCSS are necessary for college, career, and life success. Learning how to navigate across various historical text types and to analyze content by also considering text structure and source is a skill that allows students to read the multiple types of streaming videos, sound bites, newspapers, and texts exploring past and current events with an understanding of the need to integrate multiple sources when arriving at an understanding and/or position of a current event as it unfolds. In Chapter 9, we examine this developing skill set as a vehicle for engaging in social justice.

Consider how these practices are enacted as we explore two teachers embarking on using literacy learning clubs in their social studies curriculum.

## Literacy Learning Clubs in Practice: Voices from the Classroom

### Mr. P's Fifth-Grade Classroom

Mr. P is frustrated by the increasing lack of time allotted for social studies in his fifth-grade classroom. According to the curriculum, the students are supposed to be studying early U.S. history and geography, but that has been relegated to worksheets and videos at the end of the day. While Mr. P knows that he is "covering" the information, he can see by his students' affect and assessments that they are neither engaged with nor learning the content.

With the high-stakes tests in language arts and math looming and his own assessment linked to his students' success on the test, he is anxious to encroach on language arts time but sees that perhaps using literacy learning clubs with social studies content may allow him to engage students in core literacy skills while also attending to the content. Fresh from a PLC where he and other colleagues investigated the idea of disciplinary literacy, he is eager to try out this framework to transform his students' perceptions of social studies.

Mr. P decides that the unit on the Revolutionary War is a good place to pilot this approach. Instead of beginning with the textbook and facts, he turns to the themes of the NCSS to generate questions that the class will investigate using primary and secondary sources from the Revolutionary War. These themes include:

1. Culture.
2. Time, continuity, and change.

3. People, places, and environments.
4. Individual development and identity.
5. Individuals, groups, and institutions.
6. Power, authority, and governance.
7. Production, distribution, and consumption.
8. Science, technology, and society.
9. Global connections.
10. Civic ideals and practices.

The questions include:

"Who held the power?"
"How did groups work together?"
"Who were the people and places involved?"
"What was the culture of the times like?"

These four questions challenge students to investigate both the British and American perspective and, when brought together, create a comprehensive portrait of these students' understanding of the Revolutionary War that is beyond the traditional names, dates, and often singular interpretation that a textbook author offers.

Mr. P does a quick "question talk" (not unlike a book talk) around each of these core questions and invites students to rank order those they are most interested in pursuing. Mr. P then forms groups of four to five students based on interest in beginning the class's investigation of the Revolutionary War (see the Appendix for samples of how to organize choices).

Mr. P has designated 2 weeks for the project and is drawing on 40 minutes of the 90-minute language arts block to engage in the investigation. In addition to the literacy learning clubs investigation, Mr. P engages the class in a whole-class read-aloud of *The Revolutionary War: An Interactive History Adventure (You Choose: History)* by Elizabeth Raum that has the class debating, questioning, and learning about the time period by placing themselves directly in the setting of the events. The use of narrative to engage students emotionally and cognitively is well documented (Duke, 2014; Keene & Zimmermann, 2007).

Mr. P begins each learning club session with a mini-lesson specific to the needs of the group. These include:

- How to access primary source documents electronically (e.g., *http://america inclass.org/sources/makingrevolution/*).
- Methods for identifying point of view/perspective of a document.

- Strategies for locating information.
- Corroborating information across sources.
- Understanding core academic vocabulary specific to the study.
- Methods historians use to develop a multimodal presentation to share findings.

After each 10- to 15-minute mini-lesson, the groups meet to plan their work for the session and then assign individuals to tasks, which usually involve locating specific documents/texts that will help them uncover the answer to their questions. As they work, Mr. P's role shifts to that of facilitator as he mentors, coaches, reteaches, and observes the students develop a view of the questions specific to their group. Each session ends with the groups coming together (the focusing finish) to share findings and discoveries and reflect on the strategies used to engage with the content. The last five–ten minutes of their work, the think-aloud, allows Mr. P to continue to model expert thinking as he explicates the strategies he uses to navigate the multiple text types students are using in their investigations.

Each group has a shared Google Document that allows them to work on their own time as well as to locate and share findings and information. In the second week of the project, the groups move toward synthesizing their findings into a shared presentation and can choose from a variety of mediums to offer their response to the core question. Each group is required to use a mix of texts and visuals to share their findings with each other. There are a variety of tools at the groups' disposal, including cloud-based applications such as Animoto, Google Slides, and annotated screen casts. In classrooms that do not have access to the technological tools, the same task can be accomplished by creating a medium such as a pamphlet or a poster. Students are responsible for the content studied in the other group and end the work with an individual reflection on what they understand about all of the core questions as well as what they are left still wondering. This also becomes an opportunity to reflect on the literacy learning club experience itself, asking students to identify the specific literacy skills needed to complete the tasks outlined.

At the conclusion of the learning club, Mr. P believes the students have a strong understanding of the complexity of the Revolutionary War in ways that go beyond the traditional memorization of the time line. This is evidenced by the individual reflective papers students submit in which they provide an overview of the unit of study as well as reflect on the literacy learning club experience as a vehicle for learning the content. In doing so, the students have had the opportunity to develop a set of literacy tools and skills needed when looking across sources to arrive at meaning. Mr. P is hopeful that these skills will continue to be transferred in their study of social studies.

## *Ms. C's Seventh-Grade Classroom*

Ms. C has been teaching seventh-grade social studies for 15 years, and her educational background includes an undergraduate major in secondary education and history. The focus of the curriculum has always been on ancient civilizations. The class has a single textbook that takes them through the ancient civilizations, including Egypt, China, and India. Typically, the class goes through each as a unit that is predominately shaped by a whole-class lecture and individual readings and responses, with the occasional supplement of a film. The students in Ms. C's class are not very enthusiastic about the class and are often heard asking the question, "When are we ever going to use any of this?" Students perform well on assessments and complete the homework, but Ms. C is not convinced that they are actually *learning* in a way that will carry with them beyond the grade they receive in the class.

Ms. C recognizes that in this approach the content does not seem relevant to students because there is no connection. With the new CCSS in discipline-specific literacy, Ms. C recognizes the need to shift some pieces of her pedagogy. Ms. C decides to pilot literacy learning clubs for one of the units of study, Ancient Egypt, in an effort to engage students and better infuse the new standards. Ms. C begins by separating out the different subtopics of the unit. These include:

- Religion
- Habitat
- Social system
- Jobs

Typically, the students read the chapter that includes a summary of each of these subtopics and answer questions, while Ms. C adds information in her lecture. Class interaction predominantly includes a question/answer recitation from the responses at the end of the chapter, and small-group collaborations occur around those questions.

For this pilot, Ms. C introduces the students to the idea of literacy learning clubs. She explains that she is going to create "expert teams" based on interest, and instead of lecturing on content will focus more on strategies used to *access* content. The students and Ms. C are all excited to try something new. The experts, she explains, will be the students themselves as they dive into their club topic.

Ms. C begins with a brief talk on each of the subtopics of Ancient Egypt. The students then break into their teams for 2 weeks and investigate the topic. At the start of each class, Ms. C introduces and models for students how to locate sources beyond the textbook. These mini-lessons include:

- Looking at the works cited at the end of the text for additional sources
- Using media center resources to supplement learning
- Considering the different text types (e.g., video of a researcher describing findings compared to the section of the textbook) in locating information
- Looking across sources to corroborate information
- Creating an interactive presentation to share with the class

Ms. C has some reservations about this approach because while the entire class will read the text, they will only become "expert" in one area. She worries that they won't retain the same information as when they move through their traditional units of study. The learning teams schedule meetings with Ms. C—meetings that she calls guided learning sessions—to review their findings and discuss their plan for presentation. This guided learning framework gives Ms. C the opportunity to clarify misconceptions and offer opportunities for additional resources.

At the conclusion of seven class sessions (45 minutes each), the students spend the remaining 3 days putting together their final presentations. The class has access to a few computers and tables for this project, but they are not typically engaged in digital tools. Each group creates a poster presentation on their topic (though in a technology-rich classroom this can easily be done digitally), and on the 10th day the class engages in a gallery walk to learn more about the unit as a whole. Their homework assignment that evening is to write a description of what they have come to learn about the core areas of Egypt and their view of using literacy learning clubs to engage in this unit of study.

The class is generally very positive, with some recommendations for more time to investigate and to learn how to gather more resources. Ms. C is just beginning and listens to what they have to say. She looks forward to continuing to move forward, building her own understanding of the disciplinary literacy habits necessary for her students' success in social studies.

These two teachers, Mr. P and Ms. C, composites of teachers who have engaged in this type of work, reflect the philosophy that literacy learning clubs are a paradigm for instruction that must be constructed according to the content in which the teacher is positioned as well as the context in which he or she works. Rather than a recipe, it is a guideline where teachers build their unit of study around the belief that learning is social, collaborative, and inquiry based. The direction this takes will be influenced by the social studies content, the resources available, and the prior experiences of both the teachers and students. In this way, the learning of all participants continuously evolves as teachers and students engage in deep reflection about ways into the content as well as the content itself. It is a deep level of metacognition that reflects the belief that academic learning is not relegated to artificial classroom exercises and surface recall.

## Summary

Social studies instruction is inclusive of a wide range of topics, such as economics, psychology, geography, and history. According to the NCSS, in K–12 education this seemingly disparate collection of content is best organized around themes. Doing so motivates students to create a cognitive lens for understanding society and culture and the many pieces that account for these shifts over time. Generally, this is contextualized within the study of history, which if done with this approach becomes as much about the content studied as it is about developing a habit of mind for analyzing these structures.

Literacy learning clubs offer a natural paradigm for engaging students in developing this cognitive framework that motivates content learning in the discipline and creates a lens for working with content outside of the classroom. This is at the heart of civics education that underscores the development of the social sciences in K–12 education. Despite an awareness of the significance of this type of learning, little time is spent on social studies education in the elementary grades. The research and standards demonstrate the need to increase instructional time for social studies. Literacy learning clubs offer one pathway in grades 4–8 for accomplishing this goal effectively and efficiently.

## QUESTIONS FOR REFLECTION

1. What role do digital tools play in literacy learning clubs in social studies instruction?

2. In what areas of the social studies curriculum do you see this framework working to support student learning?

3. What challenges need to be considered before integrating this approach into social studies instruction?

## ACTIVITIES TO CONSIDER

- Examine the social studies curriculum you are currently asked to use. Develop a one-week (or longer, at your discretion) unit of study that invites students to use the literacy learning club paradigm to support learning. If possible, develop this unit collaboratively with a colleague so that you can support one another throughout as well as compare findings at the conclusion of the study.

- After you have engaged in this unit, consider the following:

  o What did you notice about student learning?

  o What changes will you make if you use this paradigm again?

  o How did you assess student learning?

## CHAPTER 6

# Literacy Learning Clubs in Science

The recent release of the *The Next Generation Science Standards* (NGSS; NGSS Lead States, 2013), a national effort facilitated by individual state representation calls for science education to focus on the deep understanding and application of content in ways that are transferable to what the educational community commonly refers to as college and career readiness but perhaps is best understood as *life*. The focus of these standards is on learning how to access, comprehend, and construct scientific content. This is a shift from paradigms that focus exclusively on discrete knowledge. In the executive summary, the authors note:

> Every NGSS standard has three dimensions: disciplinary core ideas (content), scientific and engineering practices, and cross-cutting concepts. The integration of rigorous content and application reflects how science and engineering is practiced in the real world.

This view of three-dimensional learning is a call for educators to see science instruction and learning as a balance of building content knowledge by developing cognitive paradigms in students that allow them to *access* the content (NGSS Lead States, 2013; see Figure 6.1).

The Standards offer this overview for educators:

> The National Research Council's (NRC) Framework describes a vision of what it means to be proficient in science; it rests on a view of science as both a body

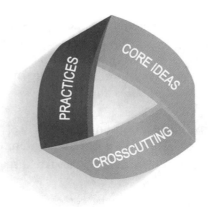

**FIGURE 6.1.** Three-dimensional learning. From NGSS Lead States (2013). Copyright ©
2013. Image used with permission from *www.nextgenscience.org.*

of knowledge and an evidence-based, model and theory building enterprise that
continually extends, refines, and revises knowledge.

Learning science should be about accessing content by developing a framework for thinking like a scientist. Educators positioned to facilitate these scientific
learning experiences need to blend content expertise with a strong understanding
of how students learn in the discipline. This requires expertise in the content and
pedagogy as well as an awareness of the literacy demands needed to access and
represent scientific information.

These standards, like many others we have seen and will investigate throughout this text, privilege developing cognitive frameworks for accessing content in
the absence of a classroom over discrete knowledge. This shift does not reflect our
typical disciplinary boundaries found in classrooms. We do not, for example, generally study themes that invite us to pull in multiple disciplines. Imagine a school
day when students' scheduled areas of study are organized by themes to investigate
rather than by disciplines. Literacy learning clubs may be a bridge that allows for
the development of these deeper cognitive frameworks while working within the
disciplinary boundaries that currently exist in schools.

In this chapter, I step inside literacy learning clubs as a tool for learning in a
science classroom that embodies this philosophy of providing tools to access the
content of the discipline, while also developing a cognitive framework for understanding the discipline outside of traditional concepts of classroom instruction.
The NRC (2012) offers this paradigm for the revision of science education in the
NGSS:

Science, engineering, and the technologies they influence permeate every aspect of modern life. Indeed, some knowledge of science and engineering is required to engage with the major public policy issues of today as well as to make informed everyday decisions, such as selecting among alternative medical treatments or determining how to invest public funds for water supply options. (p. 8)

This is at the heart of the call for authentic science instruction and learning that asks students of science to both understand the content of the discipline and develop the skills needed to independently navigate the discipline as part of their daily lives.

Science education, according to this perspective, is a much deeper and more complex endeavor than memorizing discrete facts and principles. It, much like social studies education, is an opportunity to engage in transformative ways of thinking and learning that allows participants in science education to effectively *learn* the discipline by adopting the natural habits of scientists (NGSS Lead States, 2013). The NRC (2012) goes on to offer this call to action to K–12 science educators:

> The framework is designed to help realize a vision for education in the sciences and engineering in which students, over multiple years of school, actively engage in scientific and engineering practices and apply crosscutting concepts to deepen their understanding of the core ideas in these fields. The learning experiences provided for students should engage them with fundamental questions about the world and with how scientists have investigated and found answers to those questions. Throughout grades K–12, students should have the opportunity to carry out scientific investigations and engineering design projects related to the disciplinary core ideas. (pp. 8–9)

This call for more engaged learning that connects to real-world applications prompts an opportunity to discover how the disciplines that often exist as discrete blocks of time during the school day naturally spill into each other when authentic investigations occur. As adults, we do not live our lives engaged in the world with barriers between the disciplines of literacy, social studies, science, math, and the like, but we instead draw naturally from those areas in order to engage with the activity at hand both professionally and personally. Scientists draw from math and history in their effort to make sense of the natural world around them and to create alternatives in medicine and the ecology, among others. As we turn our lenses to the other academic disciplines found in school, we find that the same is true.

If students are going to develop this conceptual framework, alternate pathways into the content must be considered. Literacy learning clubs offer a structure for engaging learners in scientific core content in ways that support the natural development of the literacy habits necessary for this deep engagement in science. In this chapter, I look specifically at how literacy learning clubs allow this deep examination of science content while constructing paradigms for accessing content. This is what I term "knowing and ways of knowing." The examples offered are designed to support elementary school teachers who are responsible for multiple subjects as well as those who are content specialists and teach multiple periods of science throughout the day.

## Disciplinary Literacy: The Literacy Lenses of Scientists

Research on the literacy habits of scientists suggests that when these experts read scientific text, their intent is to learn specific information (Fisher & Frey, 2015; Shanahan et al., 2011). When reading and writing in the sciences, there is a perpetual "weeding out" of what is new and what is known, allowing for careful, close attention to the new information. For this reason, rereading is common and often necessary before comprehension can occur. These scientists engage in similar close analysis of text when they are writing as well. Shanahan and colleagues (2011) cite the following as hallmarks of the discipline:

> Martin (1993), Veel (1997), and Wignell (1994) classified common genres of science to include (a) procedure (to provide instruction for experiments), (b) procedural recount (to record what has already been done in an experiment), (c) science report (to organize information by setting up taxonomies, parts, or steps, or by listing properties), and (d) science explanation (describing how and why phenomena occur). (p. 398)

Using academic vocabulary, the semi-technical and technical terms specific to the discipline, is an essential literacy skill for scientists, and they assume an objective stance when they are working with scientific texts (Fisher & Frey, 2015). This is in direct contrast to writers of social studies texts, which are often driven by human intention with rich narrative instead of experimental findings or reports (Draper, 2010; Fisher & Frey, 2015; Shanahan et al., 2011; Shanahan, 2015). There is also a shift in writing demands as writing in science tends to adopt the passive voice, whereas the social sciences prefer the active voice.

Analyzing text structure along with a close look at the type of academic vocabulary specific to the discipline of science provides anchors for reading as well as mentor texts for writing within the discipline. This work describes the distinct *differences* in discourse patterns when comparing science, social studies, and mathematics. This further debunks the notion that there can be a "one discipline fits all" set of literacy skills and strategies (Draper, 2010; Fisher & Frey, 2015; Shanahan et al., 2011; Shanahan, 2015). Just as in Chapter 5 where we looked at what it means to read and write like a social scientist when working within the discipline of science, we need to teach the student to read and write like a scientist when working within the sciences.

## Literacy Learning Clubs in Science Classrooms

### Literacy Learning Clubs in Elementary Science Classrooms

Science instruction, like social studies instruction, is often marginalized in the elementary grades due to the increase in high-stakes assessment in language arts and math. A longitudinal study of instructional time in classrooms in grades 1–4 shows a marked increase in time devoted to math and language arts and a gradual decrease in science and social studies instruction. While the National Center for Education Statistics (NCES) has not yet repeated this study, based on current trends it is likely that this decrease is continuing (see Table 6.1).

In addition, elementary educators often do not have academic experience in the discipline during their preservice years; few students pursuing certification in elementary education major in one of the sciences, and even if they do, much as is the case for social studies, the sciences cover a wide range of subdisciplines (chemistry, biology, physics, etc.). This consideration, coupled with the lack of methods preparation found at many institutions, creates an environment in which science is easily forgotten and at best marginalized when not dictated during a testing year.

**TABLE 6.1. Average Number of Hours of the Student School Week That Public School Teachers of Grades 1–4 Self-Contained Classrooms Spent on Each of Four Subjects: Selected Years 1987–1988 through 2007–2008**

| Subject | 1987–1988 | 1990–1991 | 1993–1994 | 1999–2000 | 2003–2004 | 2007–2008 |
|---|---|---|---|---|---|---|
| English | 11.0 | 10.5 | 10.9 | 10.9 | 11.6 | 11.7 |
| Mathematics | 4.9 | 4.9 | 5.3 | 5.7 | 5.4 | 5.6 |
| Social studies | 2.8 | 2.9 | 3.0 | 2.9 | 2.5 | 2.3 |
| Science | 2.6 | 2.7 | 3.0 | 2.6 | 2.3 | 2.3 |

*Note.* Data from U.S. Department of Education, NCES, Schools and Staffing Survey (SASS), "Public Teacher Data File," 1987–1988, 1990–1991, 1993–1994, 1999–2000, 2003–2004, and 2007–2008; "Public School Data File," 1987–1988, 1990–1991, 1993–1994, 1999–2000, 2003–2004, and 2007–2008; "Charter Teacher Data File," 1999–2000; and "Charter School Data File," 1999–2000.

When the CCSS in ELA called for more attention to nonfiction texts, the integration solution of simply inserting science texts as a piece of literacy instruction seemed an easy answer to fulfilling the requirements of attending to more nonfiction in ELA while bringing in more science content. I argue, however, that this is a solution in appearance only. The research on disciplinary literacy acknowledges that there is not one single tool kit for reading and writing that maps easily onto all disciplines (Draper, 2010; Fisher & Frey, 2015; Shanahan, 2015). Simply using science texts in the language arts block does not engage students in the deep investigation of the discipline called for by the NGSS, nor does it offer students the opportunity to develop the scientific literacy habits necessary to successfully navigate the discipline.

Many national organizations have issued a call to focus on STEM or STEAM education in the early grades to create a population of students who are engaged in the sciences and related fields and continue on to pursue careers in these areas. If we are going to cultivate this embrace of the sciences in our youngest students, we also need to invest in the educators who will be facilitating interest in these areas. While many local programs provide opportunities for this engagement, the national reform effort that is needed has yet to occur. And so the disparity continues.

## *Literacy Learning Clubs in Middle School Science Classrooms*

It is no surprise, then, that struggle and disengagement are the result when students enter middle school where they are typically engaged in science instruction daily with an instructor who has a core academic major or concentration in the content. It is a large leap for those beginning a focused study of social studies and arguably an even larger leap for many in the sciences who come to middle school without the habits of mind necessary to navigate the discipline. For many, a dislike for the subject occurs because their positive experiences have been limited. In the elementary grades, many children find themselves working with teachers who are confident in their capacity to create structures for learning but lack knowledge of the discipline. In middle school, the reverse is often true. Many middle school science teachers may have strong content knowledge but limited understanding of the appropriate literacy instruction for supporting students in the discipline. In the elementary and middle school classroom, a deep understanding of both is needed.

In addition, the research suggests that it is critical that all educators have an understanding of the discipline-specific literacy habits necessary to help these students navigate the course content. The recent integration of the CCSS for literacy in science offers a pathway for considering the literacy habits necessary for success in this discipline. These standards name the following literacy skills needed in science and the technical subjects in the middle grades. In order to cultivate this discipline-specific literacy lens, however, we need to consider integration in the elementary grades as well.

### Key Ideas and Details

CCSS.ELA-LITERACY.RST.6-8.1: Cite specific textual evidence to support analysis of science and technical texts.

CCSS.ELA-LITERACY.RST.6-8.2: Determine the central ideas or conclusions of a text; provide an accurate summary of the text distinct from prior knowledge or opinions.

CCSS.ELA-LITERACY.RST.6-8.3: Follow precisely a multistep procedure when carrying out experiments, taking measurements, or performing technical tasks.

### Craft and Structure

CCSS.ELA-LITERACY.RST.6-8.4: Determine the meaning of symbols, key terms, and other domain-specific words and phrases as they are used in a specific scientific or technical context relevant to grades 6–8 texts and topics.

CCSS.ELA-LITERACY.RST.6-8.5: Analyze the structure an author uses to organize a text, including how the major sections contribute to the whole and to an understanding of the topic.

CCSS.ELA-LITERACY.RST.6-8.6: Analyze the author's purpose in providing an explanation, describing a procedure, or discussing an experiment in a text.

### Integration of Knowledge and Ideas

CCSS.ELA-LITERACY.RST.6-8.7: Integrate quantitative or technical information expressed in words in a text with a version of that information expressed visually (e.g., in a flowchart, diagram, model, graph, or table).

CCSS.ELA-LITERACY.RST.6-8.8: Distinguish among facts, reasoned judgment based on research findings, and speculation in a text.

CCSS.ELA-LITERACY.RST.6-8.9: Compare and contrast the information gained from experiments, simulations, video, or multimedia sources with that gained from reading a text on the same topic.

### Range of Reading and Level of Text Complexity

CCSS.ELA-LITERACY.RST.6-8.10: By the end of grade 8, read and comprehend science/technical texts in the grades 6–8 text complexity band independently and proficiently. (NGA & CCSSO, 2010)

The Standards outline the types of literacy experiences Shanahan and colleagues (2011) describe in their work with scientists. These standards ask educators to support students' awareness both of content and of the text structures and academic vocabulary necessary to get at that content. This connects well with the call to position students to balance acquisition of content with the development of a cognitive framework to navigate the discipline. This calls for educators to create opportunities for students to begin to develop content knowledge while simultaneously becoming aware of the cognitive frameworks needed to learn new information.

Naming the standards, however, is not enough. A number of pieces need to be connected to create a pathway for student success beginning in the elementary grades. This is an area for professional development as we consider the many gaps in science education that interfere with student success. Use of the literacy learning club paradigm to support both teachers' and students' explicit awareness of the literacy habits necessary for success in the content is one avenue for offering access to the inquiry-based model of learning that the NGSS supports and the literacy learning club paradigm offers. For educators first embarking on this journey, collaborating with colleagues while implementing this paradigm becomes an opportunity for professional learning and understanding.

In the next section, we step inside Mr. S's fourth-grade classroom and Ms. B's sixth-grade classroom as they integrate literacy learning clubs into their science instruction. As we do so, I invite you to reflect on their efforts to link content with pedagogy in a way that is transformative for the students.

## Literacy Learning Clubs in Practice: Voices from the Classroom

### Mr. S's Fourth-Grade Classroom

Mr. S has been teaching fourth grade for 4 years and does not have a broad background in science, but he is eager to learn. Previous to this year, the science curriculum consisted of science kits (building electrical circuits, growing plants, etc.) that were meant to motivate inquiry-based learning. In practice, however, Mr. S and many of his colleagues found that they offered a scripted curriculum with rushed implementation, so while the students certainly were engaged and enjoyed the activity, he recognizes that learning was limited beyond the specific unit of study itself.

Mr. S is not confident that the students left the class with an understanding of how to investigate phenomena as scientists. In fact, since he only kept one day ahead of the students with the content, he is not certain that he has a firm understanding of these phenomena either. Science in his classroom has become a series of activities to check off a list. Mr. S realizes that in order to allow students to *learn*, more time and understanding need to be invested and students' natural questions about the world around them have to be considered.

This is easier said than done, however. Mr. S is feeling a tremendous amount of pressure to get his students ready for the state assessment in math and literacy and is torn about how to handle the call for a "deeper dive" into the discipline of science, particularly since he himself is not confident in the discipline. Mr. S was asked, however, to participate as the grade-level representative in a committee looking to integrate the NGSS into the curriculum. He was inspired by his reading of the document, and while he has questions about the implementation, scripted rubrics, and the like, he is ready to try and balance the *knowing* with *ways of knowing*. In addition, the CCSS for ELA place a greater focus on discipline-specific texts, so he feels it is now necessary and appropriate to incorporate the discipline into language arts.

Literacy learning clubs are a pathway for that "deep dive" into the content while allowing students to build their own cognitive framework for accessing content. The curriculum in fourth grade calls for a study of plants, which Mr. S, an avid gardener, had felt he had done a reasonably good job of in the past. Students grew a plant from a seed, documented growth with an observation journal, and researched how plants grow. They celebrated their work with a "plant show" for parents, complete with a written expository essay about the process. Mr. S is eager to try this new framework with an area of the science curriculum he feels comfortable with, so he gets ready in early March to launch the students into an investigation using the literacy learning clubs paradigm. In looking at this activity through the lens of what he is beginning to understand is meant by science education, he realizes that students were not deeply engaged with scientific content or processes but instead used this study as a vehicle to develop expository writing skills.

This time, instead of starting with the answer, that plants will grow and they will document the process, he is asking students to start with a question—what is the process through which growth happens? Mr. S then organizes the students into learning teams, or clubs, based on the area that they are most interested in studying. This time, however, instead of growing a seed in a Dixie cup, his students are partnering with a local farmer (a relative of one of the students in the class) to plot out a garden. "There's a lot more than science happening here," Mr. S thinks to himself. "But that's the whole point." To begin the project, the local farmer skypes with them from her farm, taking them on the tour of the land available and the dimensions. The class will periodically skype with the farmer throughout the project, as well as visit for the initial planting.

The class of 20 is organized into five groups of four. The initial task of each group is to identify potential crops that can be planted given the dimensions available, time, climate, and goal of potentially donating whatever crops are harvested. In preparation for this part of the study, Mr. S does a mini-lesson on some of the academic vocabulary used when reading about planting and models the type of reading/viewing necessary for looking for key facts within scientific texts. Students then engage in this study for two 40-minute periods using a series of bookmarked articles, videos, and their textbook. On the third day, they spend time developing their report. Prior to this development, Mr. S does a mini-lesson on creating a case study in science and demonstrates that when sharing their ideas they must include their findings and recommendations, along with their sources. Mr. S reminds the students that in science they must be able to offer evidence for their ideas as well as their findings. They submit their recommendations to the farmer, and she finalizes the list. The planned crops include:

- Potatoes
- Strawberries
- Tomatoes
- Lettuce
- Peas

New groups are then formed based on interest. Each group begins by learning more about their chosen food. The class has a good organizing start because each initial group submitted a framework that was compiled and shared via Google Docs. The groups are tasked with providing the dimensions needed for planting, the plan for growth, challenges to be aware of, and methods for harvesting. Each team has 1 week to develop this plan, which they will put together in a multi-modal presentation following the models of scientific reports they are reading. The group meets for five sessions of 40 minutes each, and Mr. S uses the literacy learning club framework to guide these meetings.

Each session begins with Mr. S providing the necessary content about the science behind plant growth as well as the strategies successful botanists adopt when working with plants. In addition, since this method of study requires that the students read multiple types of printed reports, view video clips, and navigate websites, Mr. S balances this presentation of content with study both during the focusing session and at the concluding think-aloud. During the focusing session and the think-aloud Mr. S models what he does as a reader and writer to gather and present the necessary information across these different text types. The students are reading and writing content as well as exploring methods for reading and writing in the content, which provides the opportunity to build knowledge as well as create the mental habit needed to come to that knowledge.

The team submits its recommendations to the farming staff at the local farm and then visits to launch the work with periodic site visits over the 6-week growth period, during which the team has the opportunity to observe and chart growth. Technology allows them to "visit" more frequently than the two scheduled on-site trips. At the conclusion of the project, each team writes a final report that includes recommendations for future planting based on what they learned through this initial work. The final reports are inclusive of the academic vocabulary that they have been introduced to and come to understand throughout the process. Mr. S is confident that the students have deepened their scientific knowledge of botany and have begun to develop a framework for engaging with scientific content both as readers and writers in ways that allow them to see the relevance of that knowledge to the world around them. He believes they are beginning to understand what it means to read and write like a scientist in ways that will support their learning inside the classroom and outside, too, when the heavy scaffolding he has provided throughout is not available.

The literacy learning club framework allows the learning to be designed in a way that positions the success of collaborative learning with individual accountability. Mr. S establishes the expectations and parameters of the content and context of learning, but the ability to dive deeply into the learning itself, in ways that relate beyond typical classroom exercises, creates an opportunity for the very type of scientific learning called for by the NGSS.

## Ms. B's Sixth-Grade Classroom

Ms. B has a background in chemistry and secondary education. She began her career teaching high school chemistry but has enjoyed her work in the middle school. She is passionate about her content and concerned about the apathy she sees toward science when she first meets her students in September. Ms. B has always believed in an inquiry approach to science, so she generally engages students with the curriculum through questioning, engaging in experiments, and showing examples of the content studied in the world around them. Ms. B views the text as a supplement and believes that actually engaging with science through hands-on experiences is how students learn. The challenge is and always has been resources and time.

Ms. B's students often feel frustrated by the complexity of the textbook and have a difficult time writing up their scientific work. Ms. B believes firmly that she is a science teacher and not a language arts teacher, so has generally complained about this piece of her students' work but has offered little support to them in how to improve, believing "it's not my job."

The expectations of the CCSS for science and technical subjects and now the NGSS requires her to integrate literacy in ways that support the content and help students become independent navigators of the content. The infusion of literacy learning clubs is a natural fit for her because she already values and engages in collaborative learning, and she sees that piece as the core of the approach. The new piece of the puzzle for Ms. B is being explicit through mini lessons and facilitated conversations with small groups and individuals about the literacy habits necessary to access content. This requires that she further study the literacy habits of scientists and reflect on what she does to navigate the content as a disciplinary expert. She has never really thought about *how* she reads and writes like a scientist; as a disciplinary expert, it is automatic for her. The entire sixth-grade curriculum is centered on physical science. One of the units of study is weather and erosion, and Ms. B decides to pilot this implementation with the unit of study.

Typically, Ms. B has begun with a traditional vocabulary introduction where students memorize the key terms of the unit and then engage in several experiments and analysis of photographs to understand the different principles of weathering and erosion. She concludes the unit of study with a final test before moving on to the next unit. Ms. B's students like her class because they enjoy engaging with the activities, and Ms. B is enthusiastic about the students' positive view. When asked if she believes the students are building a framework for understanding science content, she is unsure, however, because even when the students are working in small groups on experiments or field investigations, the goal is the acquisition of content, not strategies to access the content. Ms. B is uncertain if they could replicate this way of thinking without the careful scaffolding and scripted steps she provides for each group activity. Ms. B has recently attended a staff development session on using literacy learning clubs in the content areas and decides it may be worth trying to see if it helps students develop some independence when accessing scientific content.

This time, instead of beginning with the academic vocabulary of the unit, Ms. B begins by showing students video of several recent hurricanes and their impact on beaches across the United States. Without any prior knowledge, she asks the students to describe what they see and to articulate what they want to know. Ms. B then models the reading of the scientific evaluation of one of the sites presented, demonstrating how she is weeding out the pieces that do not provide a roadmap to the scientific explanation about what has been observed. Next she reads again and again those pieces that will help her put the puzzle of beach erosion together. In doing so, terms specific to the discipline come up that she teaches and she also shows resources where they can be found or understood when the context in which they are found are examined. In doing so, Ms. B is modeling "knowing and ways of knowing." It is necessary to have someone with Ms. B's disciplinary expertise model the knowledge, but it is also essential that she is explicit about the strategies she is using to access that knowledge. Central to the literacy learning club model and to what is called for in the NGSS and related documents cited earlier is this capacity for students to build both.

Ms. B then breaks down the subtopics of the unit, which include:

- Mechanical weathering
- Chemical weather
- Wind erosion
- Glacial erosion

Ms. B does a quick topic talk on each, and then groups are formed based on area of interest. Ms. B has allotted for one week of study during her 40-minute class. For the first 3 days, students will develop expertise in their area using the hands-on activities that she previously had done with all students and the related text and digital resources. On the fourth day, the students are expected to put together a digital poster that demonstrates their findings using the scientific language and reporting that they are reading throughout. On the fifth day, students will engage in a gallery walk to gather data and information on the other areas. At the start of each session Ms. B offers a 10-minute lesson on the core content of erosion as well as the strategies scientists use when reading and writing reports and conducting field experiments. Throughout, while the groups meet, Ms. B is facilitating, guiding, and at times pulling together small groups of students to reteach concepts that seem to be challenging.

Ms. B follows the framework outlined in Chapter 3 very carefully and finds that in accessing and developing materials for the think-aloud portion, she is becoming much more aware of the specific literacy habits she engages in as a scientist that she had previously taken for granted because it is so woven into her way of reading and writing and her view of the world. In doing so, she finds she is much better at articulating what students need to do to navigate the discipline—what she had previously referred to as "not my job" in ways that are of tremendous support to her students.

Instead of the typical multiple-choice test Ms. B usually gives at the end of a unit of study, the students will write an individual report titled "What Is Weathering and Erosion?" They are given specific criteria about academic vocabulary, use of scientific reporting language, and careful and clear citation of evidence from both their own investigation and from their colleagues.

Ms. B has always prided herself on creating an engaging classroom environment and believes this has allowed her to work with students individually to support growth. She recognizes, however, that the addition of the literacy lens to the discipline has afforded her the opportunity to better understand *why* students are sometimes challenged as well as to see students deepening their understanding of content. Now she is better able to offer a pathway into the content.

## Summary

Current trends in science education call for a study of content by developing a framework for accessing the content. This is a departure from traditional paradigms that focus on content knowledge, with little attention to the discipline-specific literacy habits needed to access the content. The recent call to incorporate disciplinary literacy into content areas along with the NGSS highlights the importance of helping K–12 students develop a cognitive framework for accessing scientific information. This is a shift from *knowing* and instead focuses on *ways of knowing*. As educators, this requires that we are expert both in the content and in the pedagogical structures and literacy habits needed to access the content.

Literacy learning clubs are presented in this chapter as one possible pathway for achieving the goal of content learning as well as creating schema for continuing that learning independent of the classroom. The collaborative structure mediated by focused direct instruction where needed in the content of study, as well as the literacy strategies used to access the content, provides a context where students can "try on" new knowledge and ways of getting to that knowledge with the support of peers and the expert in the classroom. In doing so, they have the opportunity to learn core scientific content while also becoming more proficient in composing, constructing, and engaging in the multiple print and nonprint text types and discourse patterns of the discipline. This second piece is what helps students develop a cognitive framework that can be used when engaging with science outside of the mediated classroom environment.

## QUESTIONS FOR REFLECTION

1. When you examine your curriculum and program of study, what role do you see for literacy learning clubs?

2. What place does science education have in your work, program, day?

3. What opportunities and challenges do you foresee when integrating this approach in your science program?

4. The NGSS have the potential to shift traditional formats for science instruction. What might be some ways we can organize the discipline of science to reflect these revised goals?

## ACTIVITIES TO CONSIDER

Work to develop one or more units of study in science using the literacy learning club paradigm. The detailed outline offered in Chapter 3 as well as the multiple resources available in the Appendix offer a roadmap for planning. It is ideal if you can plan this unit with a colleague. After you have implemented the literacy learning club in the scientific unit, reflect on the following:

- How did this paradigm support learning in this science unit?

- How did you assess student learning?

- What cognitive paradigms did you begin to see develop in your students?

- What are your thoughts about the future use of literacy learning clubs in science?

## CHAPTER 7

# Literacy Learning Clubs
# in Mathematics

The National Council of Teachers of Mathematics (NCTM) describes the need for students in K–12 to develop the capacity to move beyond surface understanding of facts, procedures, and operations toward a deeper awareness of how and why operations and facts are needed. Using their own academic vocabulary, mathematics educators who align with this perspective describe the need for "procedural fluency." The notion of fluency (much like we see it used in literacy education) suggests an automaticity and understanding that are so deep that students can transfer their knowledge of procedures to multiple contexts. The NCTM offers this perspective in its position statement on *procedural fluency*:

> Procedural fluency is a critical component of mathematical proficiency. Procedural fluency is the ability to apply procedures accurately, efficiently, and flexibly; to transfer procedures to different problems and contexts; to build or modify procedures from other procedures; and to recognize when one strategy or procedure is more appropriate to apply than another. To develop procedural fluency, students need experience in integrating concepts and procedures and building on familiar procedures as they create their own informal strategies and procedures. Students need opportunities to justify both informal strategies and commonly used procedures mathematically, to support and justify their choices of appropriate procedures, and to strengthen their understanding and skill through distributed practice. (NCTM, 2014)

A key piece of this statement is "students need experience in integrating concepts and procedures and building on familiar procedures as they create their own informal strategies and procedures." This position is very much in line with the notion of "knowing and ways of knowing" explored in the previous chapter. This approach to mathematics education, much like the other disciplines, suggests that learning math is about creating a cognitive framework or scaffold for understanding the discipline and then accessing content through that framework. This is much more sophisticated than simply memorizing core facts and procedures but arguably more in line with creating a mathematic habit of mind that links to college, career, and life readiness. This is in line with the widespread adoption of the CCSS for mathematics, representing a shift in focus from discrete skills toward more conceptual understanding. This is described in the overview of the CCSS for math:

> The Standards for Mathematical Practice describe varieties of expertise that mathematics educators at all levels should seek to develop in their students. These practices rest on important "processes and proficiencies" with longstanding importance in mathematics education. The first of these are the NCTM process standards of problem solving, reasoning and proof, communication, representation, and connections. The second are the strands of mathematical proficiency specified in the National Research Council's report *Adding It Up*: adaptive reasoning, strategic competence, conceptual understanding (comprehension of mathematical concepts, operations and relations), procedural fluency (skill in carrying out procedures flexibly, accurately, efficiently and appropriately), and productive disposition (habitual inclination to see mathematics as sensible, useful, and worthwhile, coupled with a belief in diligence and one's own efficacy). (NGA & CCSSO, 2010)

This, like the study of social studies and science explored in Chapters 5 and 6, suggests that students need to know content as well as develop a cognitive framework for accessing content, such that when presented with new information students may draw on previous understanding to begin to problem solve. This mirrors current trends and research across the disciplines suggesting that educators need to support students' capacity to demonstrate content expertise through developing a discipline-specific frame of mind for accessing and representing the content. Students also need to move beyond surface identification and recall toward deeper investigation.

Current trends in mathematics education echo the call presented in Chapters 5 and 6 that students become disciplinary experts when they create a conceptual understanding for accessing content. This perspective marks a shift from traditional views of learning math. The NCTM, in support of the CCSS, offers this position:

> The widespread adoption of the Common Core State Standards for Mathematics (CCSSM) presents an unprecedented opportunity for systemic improvement in mathematics education in the United States. The Common Core State Standards offer a foundation for the development of more rigorous, focused, and coherent mathematics curricula, instruction, and assessments that promote conceptual understanding and reasoning as well as skill fluency. This foundation will help to ensure that all students are ready for college and careers when they graduate from high school and that they are prepared to take their place as productive, full participants in society. (NCTM, 2013)

There have been differing levels of support as these new approaches are implemented in practice. This reform effort is more than just a reorganization of skills and concepts but is inclusive of a shift in the strategic use of mathematics to solve problems. The emphasis has turned to the *process* as well as the *product*. This change is in line with the notion of helping students develop the capacity to *know* and articulate *ways of knowing*. This has been a significant shift for many, particularly parents who support students and learned math in another way and did "just fine." It has created a good deal of controversy among educators and parent communities alike. Change, as we know, deep change, is hard.

There is a parallel, however, in what we are seeing across disciplines. A movement across the disciplines recognizes the need to move beyond discrete knowledge to an awareness of how knowledge is acquired. It is necessary to pair that metacognitive framework with pedagogy that supports this type of learning. It is more than just group work, and it is more than just individual practice of the concepts and ideas presented. It is using collaborative conversation and inquiry-focused learning to help students understand the importance of asking questions and then drawing on the content and collaborative context to develop independence in those areas. If we expect students to grow in this way, it will require teachers who are skilled in *both* the content of the discipline and pedagogy.

In this new model, students are using reading and writing actively in math to get at the core questions being asked and to offer insight into the process they use to arrive at the product offered. This is a highly metacognitive and sophisticated cognitive process. With the new standards, the process begins well before fourth grade as many mathematics teachers continue to respond to the question: "But if I know the answer, why do I have to explain how I got there?" It's the *explanation* that is at the heart of this new way of knowing.

It is interesting that while the CCSS for ELA explicitly name science and social studies in the 6–12 discipline-specific literacy knowledge, the name mathematics is left off of the list. Instead, the third is dubbed the technical subjects that are inclusive of computer science and mathematics. The disciplines begin to blur in ways that authentic use of information requires. Many of the standards that are described within the band of "science and technical subjects" draw attention to the complex text students must comprehend and construct when moving through the study of mathematics. Word problems are not just an exercise but an attempt to model for students the real-world application of the discrete skills and functions of math. It is as much a function of literacy as it is of mathematics. This approach is extending into study of engineering and computer science as well. The example offered in Chapter 6 of the fourth graders plotting out the farm is another example of the natural application of cross disciplines in ways that mirror real-world applications. This topic is explored in greater detail in Chapter 9.

In this chapter, I step inside literacy learning clubs as a tool for learning in a mathematics classroom. Literacy learning clubs offer a structure for engaging learners in core content in ways that support the natural development of discipline-specific literacies. In this chapter, I look specifically at how literacy learning clubs offer an avenue for the natural development of the literacy habits necessary for success in understanding mathematic content in grade 4–8 classrooms. The examples offered are designed to support elementary school teachers who are responsible for multiple subjects as well as those who are content specialists and teach multiple periods of mathematics throughout the day.

## Disciplinary Literacy:
## The Literacy Lenses of Mathematicians

This new direction in mathematics education heightens the literacy demands needed for success in the discipline. I have heard many elementary school teachers and middle school math teachers comment that success in today's math classroom is as much about reading and writing as it is about computation. The literacy skills needed to navigate mathematics include the ability to read closely and carefully to access core content and the capacity to use writing and speaking to articulate the process behind the product. Just as there are discipline-specific literacy skills needed in science and social studies, so too is that true for math (Draper, 2010). These are not generalizable but instead are specific to the texts students comprehend and create in math. Siebert and Hendrickson (2010) note:

Such texts include, but are not limited to, equations, graphs, diagrams, proofs, justifications, displays of manipulatives (e.g., base ten blocks), calculator read-outs, verbal mathematical discussions, and written descriptions of problems. For each of these types of texts, there is a specific literacy—a discipline-appropriate way of creating and interpreting a mathematical text—that students need to develop. (p. 41)

Shanahan et al. (2011, p. 406), in their study of the specific literacy habits of expert mathematicians, found that when these experts read and write in their discipline:

- Source/author of the text matters little because the focus is on the mathematics.
- Visual graphics and written words have equal value in comprehension.
- Careful, close reading weeds out unnecessary information.
- Text structure is important for both conveying and comprehending information (e.g., proofs, word problems, position of equations).

There is a language to mathematics that includes "technical" and "semitechnical" terms, commonly referred to as "academic vocabulary" (Fang, 2012; Fisher & Frey, 2015; Shanahan, 2015). *Procedural fluency*, as described above, is one example of this type of academic language.

All of the disciplines employ an academic language that is specific to the area of study that supports understanding. Research demonstrates that when students are unaware of the specific text structures and the academic vocabulary within each of the disciplines, math included, they have limited success with both the process and the product (Skinner, Pearce, & Barrera, 2016). Consider, for example, the following, from the fourth-grade CCSS in mathematics:

**Use the four operations with whole numbers to solve problems.**

CCSS.MATH.CONTENT.4.OA.A.1: Interpret a multiplication equation as a comparison, e.g., interpret $35 = 5 \times 7$ as a statement that 35 is 5 times as many as 7 and 7 times as many as 5. Represent verbal statements of multiplicative comparisons as multiplication equations. (NGA & CCSSO, 2010)

In mathematics, text is inclusive of the symbols, images, and words that are core to the discipline. In fourth grade, for example, in order to demonstrate success in the above standard, with the example provided, students need to understand the symbols (=) and (x) as well as the academic vocabulary *multiplicative, comparisons, multiplication,* and *equations*. In addition, the students must develop the capacity to articulate orally what they are reading. This is a disciplinary literacy lens that needs to be taught beginning in the elementary grades and built upon as students move up through middle school and beyond. It requires that when students approach mathematic content (both as creator and consumer), they think explicitly about the content as well as the text structure and academic vocabulary needed to access and represent the content. It means seeing all of the signs, symbols, graphs, equations, and words used when engaging in math as a text. That inclusive shift, reminiscent of the expanded definition of text investigated in Chapter 2, allows the learner to approach the content with the frame of mind necessary to uncover the *how* (process) as well as the *what* (product) that share equal importance when studying math in today's classroom.

## Literacy Learning Clubs in Math Classrooms

### *Literacy Learning Clubs in Elementary Math Classrooms*

Elementary mathematics has shifted dramatically since the adoption of the CCSS by many states and the shift in paradigm that the NCTM supports for all learners. "That's not how I was taught how to do it" is heard around many dining room tables at night (I have been guilty of saying it to my own children) as students demonstrate to parents the different processes they use to solve what used to be seen as basic math. That is because if we see mathematics as a series of processes and procedures that are mapped onto different contexts, then there is no such thing as *just* basic problem solving; instead we need to consider how these different tools are used. It requires that even when the answer is obvious, students engage in the explicit think-aloud or written explanation, so that when it is *not* so obvious they have the ability to problem solve using their understanding of content as well as process.

Similar to our discussion of science, many elementary school teachers are themselves somewhat fearful of mathematics and may stumble on some of the concepts needed. This is an area that needs to be addressed at both the preservice and professional development level so as not to translate to incorrect content being taught or to share discomfort with young children. The value in the elementary grades, however, is that there is often a greater acceptance of the value of disciplinary literacy because these teachers see how students are navigating literacy across the school day.

### *Literacy Learning Clubs in Middle School Math Classrooms*

It is here that students often become tracked by disciplines within the discipline (the text for algebra is different from that for geometry, etc.). We are therefore more likely to be working with kids already grouped by ability (like ELA) than science and social studies, which tend to be somewhat heterogeneous. Typically, the middle school students are taught by experts in mathematics, and for some, it may be the first time that they are working with someone with content expertise in this area. These math experts may have limited understanding of the role of disciplinary literacy in their content. This is an area for continued study and one that can be addressed for students through experiences such as the literacy learning club and professionally for teachers within their own professional communities (see Chapter 10 for a discussion of this topic). Literacy learning clubs motivate inquiry that is sustained and extended by the collaborative conversations that are a necessary part of integrating this model into instruction. When learners engage with new content in this inquiry-driven model that integrates social collaboration, understanding of the content deepens and there is greater retention of new knowledge. Memorizing core facts (such as the order of operations) becomes more meaningful when the need to know is driven by concrete applications (e.g., identifying the amount to spend for multiple purchases). Literacy learning clubs provide one pathway to those types of experiences.

This same deep dive into the study of the content and process that we see in the elementary grades maps onto the study of middle school mathematics as well. There is perpetual return to the core areas addressed in the CCSS in mathematics with increasing rigor and complexity, and with that comes increased text complexity. It is not unusual to have students who are expert at equations but only minimally successful with word problems. Is that a math problem? Is that a reading problem? To try and place the challenge in one camp simplifies the issue. It *is* a mathematics challenge, just as it *is* a reading challenge, because the specific literacy habits noted above are necessary for success within the discipline in class in an effort to successfully navigate mathematics for college and career readiness, *life*.

The opportunity to see the connections to occupations such as engineering and architecture offers the necessary bridge that brings these skills to life. Just as has occurred in science with the push toward building STEM or STEAM programs at the local level, we are in the midst of a national push in the "M" part of that acronym as well. Programs in robotics and the integration of science and math concepts are offering students the chance to realize how a deep understanding of the discipline, along with the text structures needed to navigate the discipline, must occur simultaneously. For example, you cannot complete computer programming or coding without also understanding the text structure behind that program. There are natural ways this engages and excites children in the elementary and middle grades with connections to creating video games, national day of coding, building and programming Legos, and so on. Unfortunately, however, these programs often exist as isolated experiences, electives, clubs, or tuition- or grant-based after-school experiences. What if these types of programs were to come into the classroom regularly? An unfortunate misrepresentation of the CCSSM and high stakes assessments such as the Partnership for Assessment of the Readiness for College and Careers (PARCC) has led some to move more toward skill and drill when at the heart of these recommendations is the effort to make learning come to life by infusing a deep study of math in ways that fully answer students' question, "When are we going to use this again?"

Much like our study of science, literacy learning clubs can become a place where using the inquiry model of learning can support students' deep understanding of the content—the "big ideas" that can only be understood by linking multiple math processes together (Bulgar, 2003). I have seen firsthand from Sylvia Bulgar's work with preservice teachers and their translation of that to practice how organizing inquiry around "big ideas" that get at the connections across mathematic processes supports students learning (Charles, 2005, p. 10). Charles offers this definition: "A Big Idea is a statement of an idea that is central to the learning of mathematics, one that links numerous mathematical understandings into a coherent whole" and includes examples such as the following (p. 10):

> **PROPERTIES: For a given set of numbers there are relationships that are always true, and these are the rules that govern arithmetic and algebra.**
>
> **Examples of Mathematical Understandings:**
>
> *Properties of Operations*
>
> - Properties of whole numbers apply to certain operations but not others (e.g., The commutative property applies to addition and multiplication but not subtraction and division.).
> - Two numbers can be added in any order; two numbers can be multiplied in any order.
> - The sum of a number and zero is the number; the product of any nonzero number and one is the number.
> - Three or more numbers can be grouped and added (or multiplied) in any order.
>
> *Properties of Equality*
>
> - If the same real number is added or subtracted to both sides of an equation, equality is maintained.
> - If both sides of an equation are multiplied or divided by the same real number (not dividing by 0), equality is maintained.
> - Two quantities equal to the same third quantity are equal to each other.

Attaining the ability to articulate this "big idea" requires a deep dive into both the content and processes needed to access the content. It requires an awareness of basic operations as well the ability to decode text structure, symbols, and associated text with the concepts and the capacity to see the relationship among sometimes disparate sections of study. Literacy learning clubs become a tool to support this type of analytic reasoning because it invites collaborative inquiry into the process in ways that motivate understanding how to use math skills to problem solve across a variety of contexts.

## Literacy Learning Clubs in Practice: Voices from the Classroom

### Ms. C's Fourth-Grade Classroom

Ms. C has been teaching fourth grade for 10 years and has always found teaching math to be a challenge. She feels confident with the content, but her students generally are not excited about the subject. Typically, they use a textbook and workbook with unit tests at the end, and as a dynamic teacher, Ms. C recognizes that, unlike the other subjects she is responsible for, the math curriculum is somewhat dry. Ms. C does not find the instruction she uses for math to be particularly engaging for students.

This year, Ms. C has the opportunity to pilot new pedagogical approaches to teach the core components of the math curriculum. She is planning on trying a variety of collaborative and workshop models to identify potential strategies for engaging students with the content and will present her findings to her colleagues at the end of the school year. These data will be used to help shape the curriculum revision that will take place during the summer. In essence, Ms. C is not changing content; there are clear guidelines in the CCSS in math that students are responsible for learning (see below). Instead, she is investigating new ways to access the content to support learning.

In fourth grade, students are expected to engage in the following:

In Grade 4, instructional time should focus on three critical areas: (1) developing understanding and fluency with multi-digit multiplication, and developing understanding of dividing to find quotients involving multi-digit dividends; (2) developing an understanding of fraction equivalence, addition and subtraction of fractions with like denominators, and multiplication of fractions by whole numbers; (3) understanding that geometric figures can be analyzed and classified based on their properties, such as having parallel sides, perpendicular sides, particular angle measures, and symmetry. (NGA & CCSSO, 2010)

In previous years, Ms. C would go through each standard within fourth grade as a unit of study broken down into the discrete skills necessary for success. A significant amount of academic vocabulary and written explanation is at the core of each of these, and students often struggle to articulate the rationale behind the processes. Ms. C wonders if this is because doing things like solving fractions or plotting geometric shapes seemed abstract and unrelated to anything outside of the worksheet.

Ms. C wants her students to be able to identify both the content and the process and wonders if beginning with a "big idea" that she has learned about through a professional development session will expand students' capacity to engage in the deep level that is being asked. The rationale is that students will better understand new concepts if the links to what they already know are made clearer. This becomes even more relevant when seen in concrete ways in the world around them.

Ms. C begins the unit that is typically "Geometry" with this question:

"I am trying to decide a method for maximizing our space in the classroom in each subject. What design can you offer, along with an explanation of why this design is useful?"

- Language arts
- Math
- Social studies
- Science

Students are organized into four groups based on the content area for which they are interested in designing the learning space.

To be successful, students need:

- To acquire the academic vocabulary of geometry
- To learn the principles of measurement
- To identify geometric shapes and recognize their use in the environment
- To be able to read the different texts (e.g., measurement, vocabulary) and write using those same terms

Ms. C decides to devote 10 instructional class periods using the literacy learning clubs design. Ms. C begins each 40-minute session with a mini-lesson on the above features. These mini-lessons involve her reading aloud design documents that make use of these principles in relevant architecture and design work. It also involves the explicit teaching of the mathematical concepts, such as measurement and representation as well as design.

After each mini-lesson, the teams of students (four to five in a group) meet to review the concepts studied and to assign individual tasks for 15 minutes of investigation. This meeting involves, among other things, reading and reviewing materials by designers in an effort to understand how professionals conceive of using the different spaces. It also includes using digital sources to review concepts introduced as well as the textbook. Interestingly, as students are designing how to use the space for the different disciplines, Ms. C is beginning to understand a lot about her students' perspectives on how learning occurs in these different content areas. Throughout, Ms. C takes an active role in mediating conversations, motivating thinking by asking focused questions, and, at times, pulling together small groups to reteach skills as needed. The group then meets to share findings and begin to draft their ideas visually as well as an annotated list. Student groups have the option of either designing on the computer or using traditional paper/pencil and graph paper. Each session always ends with Ms. C's "think-aloud" as she articulates the way she is decoding or working with mathematical text or geometric representations. On one day it is an opportunity for her to model scale, something she has introduced during an earlier focusing session. This is an opportunity to revisit a complex topic.

On the fifth day the students get ready to put together their proposal. For this mini-lesson, Ms. C models the different pieces of a proposal. The proposal must include the visual design map that is proportionally represented with appropriate labeling of geometric shapes and a rationale for inclusion. In addition, there needs to be a written explanation of how the proposal was developed and how it meets the needs of the task. Ms. C reminds the class that when reviewing their work, they need to ensure that the mathematical representations are accurate to ensure the design is appropriate. The class will be checking for these with one another as well.

Day 8 involves a gallery walk as teams review one another's proposals based on the guidelines Ms. C established on day 5. The goal is for the group to comment on the proposals. Once completed, the proposals are shared with the entire class where there is further opportunity to analyze findings, offer input, and revise. As part of this sharing, which involves the development of digital presentations, Ms. C talks with the class about how to present using academic vocabulary, and she models several examples so that they understand not only how to construct the mathematical explanation but also how to talk about it to others. The capacity to explain concepts to others demonstrates comprehension and sustains learning. As teachers, think of how many times one of us has had the experience that we did not fully understand a topic or concept until we were put in the position of having to help someone else understand. The ability to articulate new knowledge is a powerful piece of the learning puzzle. At the conclusion, the group decides which design proposals to implement in the classroom to best support learning throughout the school day.

Ms. C's work is an example of how literacy learning clubs can be integrated into a math program to support overall goals. The above project provides lots of opportunity to grow the work. At the heart of these collaborative investigations is the students' ability to learn the core content (in this case, geometry and measurement) by engaging in the natural literacy demands that are specific to mathematics, including reading and composing either digitally or through traditional approaches using inquiry as a way to deepen expertise. As students begin to see how previously discrete concepts in math are connected and as engagement deepens, their expertise grows.

## Ms. K's Eighth-Grade Classroom

Ms. K has an academic background in mathematics and secondary education and has been teaching eighth grade for 5 years. The students are grouped based on ability in the middle school, and Ms. K works primarily with those identified as in need of academic support. These students generally struggle in both math and language arts and are not enthusiastic about school. Ms. K believes that the district push toward *more* skill and drill for this population of students is not effective. She decides to pilot literacy learning clubs as a way to engage students and deepen their learning.

The class Ms. K is working with has 16 students in an effort to support their very individual needs. In general, in eighth grade, the standards-driven curriculum requires the following:

> In Grade 8, instructional time should focus on three critical areas: (1) formulating and reasoning about expressions and equations, including modeling an association in bivariate data with a linear equation, and solving linear equations and systems of linear equations; (2) grasping the concept of a function and using functions to describe quantitative relationships; (3) analyzing two- and three-dimensional space and figures using distance, angle, similarity, and congruence, and understanding and applying the Pythagorean Theorem. (NGA & CCSSO, 2010)

Linear equations have always been challenging for her students, particularly this group, and have become even more challenging when the students use a word problem to develop the equation and solve. Ms. K is unsure whether the difficulty stems from lack of math knowledge or from reading confusion, but as she engages more with the notion of disciplinary literacy, it becomes clear that it is not an either/or situation but a need to support students' work in both areas.

Ms. K begins the unit of study with focused, explicit instruction on linear equations. Using a workshop approach, she offers 10 to 15 minutes of direct instruction with extensive modeling and then confers with students individually to assess understanding. Generally, after students understand the concept and math involved, she moves on to word problems that ask students to represent equations and solve. It is here that challenges often begin, so she decides to adopt a different approach. Instead, she begins with a real scenario, developed in collaboration with the principal, to build up this skill in a relevant and useful way. The workshop approach has been helpful in supporting individual learning, but she recognizes that the students still fail to see the connection to how this knowledge is helpful outside of the classroom.

Ms. K announces to the class that the students will be responsible for organizing the resources for the upcoming school carnival. Multiple areas need to be organized, including:

- Food
- Prizes
- Budget

Ms. K explains that they have to keep a variety of unknown variables in mind as they put this together; thus, the goal is to set up equations that will allow them to present a variety of options. Ms. K forms groups based on area of interest, and the students have 3 days to develop a plan for their area and then come together to create a proposal for the principal.

Ms. K directs the students to a variety of digital resources that demonstrate the real-world application of linear equations. She models the way she approaches the following word problems[*] as a reader and mathematician to make decisions about real-life events:

1. A teacher is trying to determine whether she can afford a new set of classroom calculators for $300 and still purchase school supplies for all of her students. If the cost per student for supplies is $9.75, a linear equation can be constructed to show the total cost, expressed as *y,* for any number of people

---

[*] Word problems developed by Lindsay Kenyon, middle school math teacher, and used with permission.

in her class, $x$. The linear equation would be written as $y = 9.75x + \$300.00$. With this equation, the teacher can substitute any number of students and determine the total amount she will have to spend.

2. A teacher is trying to determine whether or not she can afford school supplies for all of her students. If the price per person for math supplies is $\$9.75$, a linear equation can be constructed to show the total cost, expressed as $y$, for any number of people in her class, $x$. The linear equation would be written as $y = 9.75x$. With this equation, the teacher can substitute any number of students and determine the total cost of supplies for all students.

Ms. K models how, as a reader, to extrapolate the necessary information and the use of symbols to signify the unknown and how, as a writer, she will represent that information. This requires a level of careful, close reading that she has always understood is necessary for success in mathematics but has not explicitly modeled or discussed with students until now.

The groups work to first identify resources and begin by referring back to data from past carnivals, which gives them access to approximate attendance, cost of ticket, and past budgets, among other data. They refer frequently to examples such as the one that Ms. K provides to see how to set up the equation to offer the answers needed. As Ms. K circulates and works with the students, she notices that the academic vocabulary such as equation and symbol, which previously eluded students because they seemed so abstract, are much more accessible to the group now because the focus is on the very popular carnival and the mathematics is becoming a tool to support their work.

At the conclusion of 3 days, the groups share their work with Ms. K and the principal and model the number of ways the equations developed can be used to calculate cost and resources in the areas identified. They have created a shared Google Document that allows the work to be distributed as needed and modified by many. Their equations are not perfect, and when working with real numbers in their own environment, they revise them based on input.

This is an example of a short-term use of literacy learning clubs to support student learning. Ms. K sees that at the conclusion of this 3-day activity students have a much deeper understanding of the content and processes because both were developed in relation to one another using the collaborative investigation that supports student learning. Engagement is key to the learning that takes place, and Ms. K is looking forward to expanding this approach in the classroom.

# Summary

Current trends in mathematics education are focusing on developing conceptual understandings instead of discrete memorization. Students arrive at accuracy by developing a cognitive framework for the process needed to arrive at products. This ability to *know* and articulate *ways of knowing* requires an examination of the reading and writing processes needed to arrive at and demonstrate understanding. Literacy learning clubs offer a paradigm for the examination of mathematics content through the unique disciplinary literacy lens that mathematicians adopt when working with content. Helping students understand these specific processes has the potential to make the content more engaging and the learning more sustainable because it is rooted in authentic applications.

The examples presented in this chapter demonstrate that the literacy learning club paradigm can be bound in specific ways and durations depending on the needs of the students and teachers. In Ms. C's fourth-grade classroom, the literacy learning club framework integrates an extended unit of study over 2 weeks, while in her eighth-grade classroom Ms. K chooses a more focused unit that initially requires three 40-minute periods of study. The learning club framework is designed to offer a way of structuring learning in both the short and long term and should be adapted and adjusted based on the unique context in which the teacher and students are positioned.

## QUESTIONS FOR REFLECTION

1. Mathematics is often seen as the subject that is most challenging to integrate. Is that a fair description? What possibilities do you see for literacy learning clubs in mathematics?

2. What are the challenges and possibilities for integration?

3. Where in your curriculum can the literacy learning club approach be used to support student learning?

## ACTIVITIES TO CONSIDER

Review your current math curriculum. Identify a place where literacy learning clubs may be used to support student learning. Develop a short-term use of these to pilot how this model may support your students' learning. If possible, collaborate with a colleague throughout. At the conclusion of this unit of study consider the following:

- How did students engage with the material differently than when using traditional forms of math instruction?
- How well did students come to learn the curricular expectations?
- How else might you use this paradigm in math in the future?
- What would you change for the next time? What would you retain?

## CHAPTER 8

# Literacy Learning Clubs in Special Areas

In this chapter, I step inside literacy learning clubs as a tool for learning in special areas. In Chapters 5–7, I explored literacy learning clubs as a structure for engaging learners in core content in ways that support the natural development of discipline-specific literacies. In this chapter, I look specifically at how literacy learning clubs offer an avenue for the natural development of the literacy habits necessary for success in what is often described as the "special" areas. Specifically, I look at physical education, art, music, and business/technology education since they have a history of being offered in K–12 schools, but as we delve into these disciplines the boundaries around them become blurred.

Studying a single discipline at a time is somewhat artificial, for it seems to suggest that any other areas studied in school do not fall within this disciplinary literacy camp. That is in part due to the challenge of creating boundaries between subjects. In some ways, the recent revisions to the core standards across disciplines, along with positions taken by the associated professional organizations, ask educators to do the impossible because our schools are designed around the principle that knowledge is defined by discipline. How do we integrate STEM or STEAM when math and science are taught separately? How can we consider the social sciences as a pattern of themes when students move from American history to world history in their study? These are important questions that we need to continue to ask, but as new technologies and new literacies push us into different ways of thinking about learning, it is necessary to consider how that can be balanced in the current structures available to educators and children.

Recognizing that literacy is inclusive of all content that students navigate daily becomes a bridge to seeing this work as integrated into the world in which we are preparing children to enter as adults. It ushers in a natural view of what it means to be "college and career ready." I invite you to engage in thinking through the disciplinary literacy habits necessary for success in the disciplines studied in this chapter and the possibilities literacy learning clubs offer in these areas to consider how this may be mapped on to other areas of study—perhaps some we have yet to even imagine bringing into the school day. This framework transitions into the next chapter, which examines literacy learning clubs as a paradigm for getting students involved with current social issues, specifically helping students to develop an awareness of these social issues and to provide the relevant academic tools needed to become an active participant in social justice matters.

## Literacy Habits Outside of the Core Content Disciplines

Our K–12 descriptors of what counts as the core disciplines and what are seen as "specials" suggest an artificial hierarchy that is in some ways being replicated in my decision to focus on multiple areas within a single chapter. In 1859, Herbert Spencer asked the question, "What knowledge is of most worth?" Educators have continued to grapple with that question ever since as we work within the structures of time and scheduling that impose demands that, at times, are at odds with our beliefs about learning.

Draper and colleagues make a case for the literacy needs in all of these areas, those described as "core content," as explored in the previous chapters and "specials" such as art, music, and physical education, among others and I concur (Draper, 2010; Fisher & Frey, 2015). In the interest of space, however, we negotiate multiple subjects within this chapter in an effort to show that discipline-specific literacies extend throughout the school day as it currently exists in practice. These subjects are organized not by subject area but by what links them together, including specialists in movement, music, visual production, and business/technology education. The chapter concludes with "Voices from the Classroom" to put these ideas into practice.

In many ways, this is as much an education for the teachers of these disciplines as it is a way to build awareness in students. The specialists in these areas often see the literacy piece as removed from the work that they do with children, and often marginalized, they find themselves in the position of continuously advocating for their "noncore," "nontested" subject area and students. These are the areas that are often first hit by budget cuts and reduction in space and last serviced by new materials and program. When we consider our expanded definition of literacy offered in the earlier chapters, which is inclusive of fixed and moving images and asks us to read the world around us as much as the words in front of us, we begin to see how the literacy lens of these disciplines is essential to success across all content areas (Freire & Macedo, 1987). In addition, as we work within these areas, the need to pull in skills from the core content disciplines discussed earlier is clear. As students build a cognitive awareness of these intersections, they deepen their content expertise in all areas.

## Movement (Physical Education and Dance)

Literacy is woven into each of the national standards in physical education (Society of Health and Physical Education [SHAPE], 2013). Literacy in this context is understood as the capacity to understand and develop movement in ways that invite health and well-being.

### National PE Standards

SHAPE America's National Standards define what a student should know and be able to do as [a] result of a quality physical education program. States and local school districts across the country use the National Standards to develop or revise existing standards, frameworks and curricula.

**Standard 1**—The physically literate individual demonstrates competency in a variety of motor skills and movement patterns.

**Standard 2**—The physically literate individual applies knowledge of concepts, principles, strategies and tactics related to movement and performance.

**Standard 3**—The physically literate individual demonstrates the knowledge and skills to achieve and maintain a health-enhancing level of physical activity and fitness.

**Standard 4**—The physically literate individual exhibits responsible personal and social behavior that respects self and others.

**Standard 5**—The physically literate individual recognizes the value of physical activity for health, enjoyment, challenge, self-expression and/or social interaction.

The field of dance shares this belief that movement is a text, a narrative to construct and comprehend. Seeing the narrative told in the visual representation of the arts is not new. The explicit awareness of the way we decode and create movement in an effort to convey information is a form of disciplinary literacy, in this case reading body movement and understanding how to use movement to convey a message. It is much more than simply keeping a journal of what you do in movement-related fields. Instead, it is developing an understanding of how the movements become a text themselves.

The construction and comprehension of this information can be understood on multiple levels. Learning to read and use body language, for example, is an essential component of communication. Similarly, in these fields that are so closely aligned with health and nutrition sciences, there is also a connection to understanding how to decode and apply nutrition and health information located within the environment to support overall well-being.

As we begin to consider the application to these related fields, disciplines begin to blend. Isn't the decoding of nutrition labels math? Does telling the narrative of a nonverbal dance parallel comprehending fiction in language arts? The answer to both questions is yes, and that is what is key to the pathway of learning that literacy learning clubs are meant to invite. The discipline-specific barriers we place on our school day are artificial. We do not operate in a discipline-specific world, rather we solve real problems and engage in real scenarios and then draw on relevant expertise that is at its core cross disciplinary. The connection is the capacity to draw upon the relevant strategies specific to the areas located in math, science, social studies, the arts, and so on, which allows the participant to construct and comprehend the texts. When we enter into a dance performance, we are not following a sequence chain in the way we navigate an equation. Instead we are pairing the text of movement, often music, within the context of where it is represented to understand the information being conveyed or the narrative being woven. These things can happen naturally, almost without awareness of what we are doing cognitively. If we make explicit the strategies used when decoding and creating movement narratives or reading about nutrition, students in the upper elementary and middle school grades will begin to build an awareness of how we engage in disciplinary literacy outside of what is traditionally seen as academic. It is the path for unlocking the discipline when we begin to decode the mystery behind the magic.

## Music

Music parallels math in the use of symbols to construct and convey meaning. Additionally, the academic vocabulary of tone, pacing, among others, becomes key to the goal of becoming both a composer and a listener. The verbal and the nonverbal are pieces of this literacy puzzle. Broomhead (2010) suggests that musical literacy "may be defined broadly as the ability to interact (perform, listen, contemplate, and create) appropriately with musical texts. Meaning-making comes through discipline-appropriate negotiation and creation of these texts. Music texts may include words but usually involve resources that are quite independent from written language" (p. 70). Approaching upper elementary and middle school instruction in the requisite music class from the lens of decoding the text of the discipline offers an opportunity for students to experience the content in ways that put them in charge of the experience.

The National Association for Music Education (NAfME, 2014) recently revised the national standards to reflect this shift from knowledge acquisition to an awareness of process. Like the movement standards, the music standards acknowledge the expanded definition of literacy presented in this text, as they call for educators to support students' development of music literacy. In the rationale, the organization acknowledges:

> **The 2014 Music Standards are all about *Music Literacy*.** The standards emphasize conceptual understanding in areas that reflect the actual processes in which musicians engage. The standards cultivate a student's ability to carry out the three Artistic Processes of
>
> - Creating
> - Performing
> - Responding
>
> These are the processes that musicians have followed for generations, even as they connect through music to their selves and their societies. And isn't competence in Creating, Performing, and Responding what we really want for our students?
>
> *Students need to have experience in creating, to be successful musicians and to be successful 21st century citizens.*
> *Students need to perform—as singers, as instrumentalists, and in their lives and careers.*
> *Students need to respond to music, as well as to their culture, their community, and their colleagues.*

Current trends in music education call for students to develop "music literacy" by creating, performing, and responding to music as text. These trends parallel the belief studied throughout this text that learning happens when students have the opportunity to create cognitive frameworks for accessing content. Music, like the other disciplines studied, is better explored when students move beyond recall and recognition and have opportunities to explore the development and construction. It deepens the experience and supplies students with a lens that contributes to their work with music outside of the school setting. This approach supports the development of a conceptual framework that invites students to deconstruct the discipline as they build an awareness of "ways of knowing" that strengthens the capacity to fully engage with the discipline outside of the school experience.

## Production (Visual Arts, Theater, and Media)

Similarly, in the production arts where students are creating images, pieces, and even food artifacts, the opportunity to blend multiple disciplines for a particular goal arises. In addition, there is the literacy of the field itself. Jensen, Asay, and Gray (2010) note, "Good art teachers engage their students in the talk, tools, techniques and processes inherent to each art text to help students understand and use each of these texts." This is an understanding of genre, period, as well as the capacity to read the visual.

Interestingly, just as in music education when the 1994 standards were revised in 2014 to create a deeper awareness of music literacy, so too did the national arts standards that are inclusive of dance, media arts, theater and visual arts undergo a deep revision in 2014. It seems that the evolution of the CCSS for math and ELA led to other disciplines examining the ways in which they were asking educators and children to engage with content. Dance is a discipline that falls within both the domain of physical education/movement and the arts. These revised standards also ask students to create, perform, and respond to artistic texts, with a fourth component to *connect* to the context in which the art is created (National Coalition for Core Arts Standards [NCCAS], 2014). The rationale for the standards offers this framework for engaging with the arts in K–12 education:[*]

> . . . these new, voluntary National Core Arts Standards are framed by a definition of artistic *literacy* that includes philosophical foundations and lifelong goals, artistic processes and creative practices, anchor and performance standards that students should attain, and model cornerstone assessments by which they can be measured. The connective threads of this conceptual framework are designed to be understood by all stakeholders and, ultimately, to ensure success for both educators and students in the real world of the school. (NCCAS, 2014, p. 2, emphasis added)

Once again *literacy*, the idea of constructing and creating meaning, is explicit within the discipline of study. Study in the arts parallels the other disciplines

---

[*]National Core Arts Standards © 2015 National Coalition for Core Arts Standards. Rights administered by State Education Agency Directors of Arts Education (SEADAE). All rights reserved. *www.nationalartsstandards.org.*

investigated throughout the text that ask participants to engage with the study in ways that allow the students to become contributors, *readers and writers* in this expanded understanding of literacy, and not just observers, as previous iterations of work within the discipline have suggested.

We can continue to extend this rationale to all sorts of opportunities to construct and create, including cooking and food science, which also blend to include mathematics and science as a way of working within the discipline. As we navigate this path of creating cognitive structures for reading and writing, the word and world around us, the disciplines continue to blur.

## Business and Technology Education

Business education assumes responsibility for supporting students' personal and professional sense of economic principles and financial literacy. In addition, the field is also becoming increasingly responsible for students' awareness of trends in technology. The field has shifted as society has moved away from the study of typing and systems for capturing information to investigating the financial and technological literacies (now referred to as information technology) needed for college and career readiness. In the National Standards for Business Education (National Business Education Association, 2007) the organization notes:

> In classrooms nationwide, business educators play a prominent role in preparing students to become responsible citizens, capable of making the astute economic decisions that will benefit their personal and professional lives. Using the concepts described in these standards, business teachers introduce students to the basics of personal finance, the decision-making techniques needed to be wise consumers, the economic principles of an increasingly international marketplace, and the processes by which businesses operate. In addition, these standards provide a solid educational foundation for students who want to successfully complete college programs in various business disciplines.
>
> This collection of national standards is a forward-looking synthesis of what students should know and be able to do in business.
>
> The standards are based on a vision and a set of competencies designed to prepare students to become knowledgeable and ethical decision makers as they fulfill their roles as consumers, workers, and citizens.

The discipline of business education includes accounting, business law, career development, communication, computation, economics and personal finance, entrepreneurship, information technology, international business, management, and marketing. While the focused study typically begins in high school, it is not unusual to see this woven into middle school programs and connected to the core disciplines of English, social studies, and math in the upper elementary grades.

## Creating Connections: Linking These Fields to Literacy Learning Clubs

The areas studied in this chapter often dubbed the "specials" spill into the traditional core disciplines both in content and in types of reading and writing needed to access the information. The same careful close reading needed to negotiate word problems in mathematics is necessary when reading and constructing computer programs, for example. The rich understanding of narrative connected to specific contexts required to navigate the social sciences and ELA is also engaged when developing music and art literacy. The focus is on developing the conceptual framework for exploring these diverse literacy experiences and constructing appropriately within the domain. The emphasis is on understanding how to access and construct text and not on discrete recall or artificial academic designations.

Literacy learning clubs allow us to work within the academic structures while building students' capacity to engage with text in its multiple forms and its multiple disciplines naturally and in ways that make sense beyond the classroom experience. Adopting this framework, we focus on the value of metacognition because, in order for students to negotiate these disciplines, they must approach all learning as a text to be studied through deconstruction, construction, and sometimes reconstruction. The students come to the content through a deep understanding of the core literacy habits necessary for studying the specific discipline. It is an exciting and engaging way to learn. Specifically, it balances current structures of schools with recent trends across the content areas, moving away from a view of learning as discrete blocks of information to consume to a view where everyone is actively constructing all of the time. This shift is very much connected to the world in which we live where information is just a point and click away. Our work is to create the cognitive awareness of how to integrate that information into our work within the world we live. This issue is investigated further in Chapter 9.

The disciplines discussed in this chapter that exist outside of the traditional core academic content embody a set of discipline-specific literacy skills that ask students to consider the habits of mind necessary to understand the content. In that way, it is quite similar to our study inside the core disciplines because the emphasis is on "knowing" as well as developing "ways of knowing." Art class, for example, should help students develop a framework for understanding the construction and comprehension of images in ways that are linked to the context in which they are created. Physical education becomes an opportunity for students to develop healthy life habits. In both of these examples, and in the other disciplines discussed in this chapter, the class becomes the place where students study the skills that they can apply outside of school.

As mentioned in the introduction, the barriers we place between disciplines in schools are somewhat artificial. For literacy learning clubs to come alive in these disciplines, we need to consider the focus of inquiry and then allow students to draw on the natural literacy habits necessary to move forward as learners. We need to inspire students to study music forms by first giving them the opportunity to hear different types and then let their interest drive the period of study. We can do the same for the visual and performing arts. It is here that the content specialists become facilitators of the academic discourse of their discipline. Even as I write this text, this chapter in particular, as I try to create boundaries to define how literacy learning clubs can support study in specific disciplines, I see natural and necessary blending into others. The hope is that students begin to see that relationship, as well as the study of academic content and discourse, as relevant and purposeful and not as abstract and disparate, as so many students voice in the upper elementary and middle school grades. In Chapter 9, we break down these walls even further as we look inside the value of integrating literacy learning clubs for social justice.

## Literacy Learning Clubs in Practice: Voices from the Classroom

### *Music with a Mission*

Music has a long history of revolution; we can point to songs across history that represent an ideology or position, an opportunity to give voice to a way of thinking and believing. Studying *revolution* in a middle school class through this lens invites students to look at music with a critical eye and to *read* music as a text that is part of a larger narrative.

We were discussing music in class the other day, and Tiara, one of my students, likened this type of study to peeling away the layer of an onion; looking to find the complexities that underscore the surface of the work.

Students begin class by listening to music and looking at lyrics (for songs that have them) as a way of understanding the perspective. They naturally consider tone, tempo, and the context surrounding production, and they investigate the author of songs with lyrics and the composer and so begin to uncover something about their historical position.

Mapping this inquiry-based study of music within the learning club paradigm offers an opportunity for educators to frame this study around the lenses needed to understand music, thereby creating a paradigm that transforms students' ways of experiencing music. Now, as students sit beside the music, they consider the text, composer, and context in which it developed. This is the goal of the literacy learning club: to provide an inquiry-based framework that allows students to develop the literacy lenses needed for successfully understanding the content. They become expert in content by learning the cognitive frameworks necessary for learning within the discipline—all disciplines.

## *Creating a Collage for Children*

Visual art is a medium that has long held content in its visual image. National standards in ELA have called for including the visual, both moving and fixed, as part of the literacy investigation. Investigating this medium as an artist offers an alternate lens for using disciplinary literacy as a pathway for negotiating the content. The NAEA (National Association for Education in the Arts; available at *https://www.arteducators.org/about*) offers this vision in the 2014 construction of standards:

> Students of all ages benefit from comprehensive, balanced, and sequential learning in the visual arts, led and taught by qualified teachers who are certified in art education. Art educators meet ethical and rigorous standards of excellence in preservice preparation, ongoing professional development, pedagogy, and inquiry in the field. School-based visual arts instruction surpasses national, state, and local standards and is enhanced through access to art museums and other community resources. The power of the visual arts to enrich human experience and society is recognized and celebrated throughout the world.

In many ways, the process of developing a visual representation closely parallels the work of authors in that the artist first decides the genre and message and then creates the narrative using the visual representation as the medium. Helping students deconstruct this process and use these lenses both when creating and comprehending visual mediums strengthens the awareness and understanding of fine art from the perspective of both artist and interpreter.

The recent interest in "makerspaces," discussed in Chapter 2, puts students in the position of enacting these possibilities. Students become artists and engineers as they work with materials to create something new. Using the literacy learning club paradigm allows students to work collaboratively around core topics of investigation selected in consultation with the teacher who represents the call in arts education to move from study of the form to actively creating, performing, responding, and connecting. Consider the possibilities and the opportunities outside of the special areas to integrate this type of learning experience.

## Summary

Disciplinary literacy is inclusive of the special areas that are often relegated to nonacademic places in the school day (physical education, art, technology education, among others). The view of disciplinary literacy as a pathway to learning actively resists this perspective. Designations of these areas as nonacademic are arbitrary and reflect an outdated philosophy that compartmentalizes education and learning into a hierarchy of discrete knowledge. While this model is orderly and organized in our current information age where knowledge is readily available, this is not helpful.

Instead, all of these fields task us, as educators, with helping students create the capacity to work within the discipline as a way to understand the content. In the process, we are creating lasting conceptual frameworks that allow students to understand, for example, music and theater, even if it is not their professional field, long after the classroom study has ended. Literacy learning clubs provide a framework for this type of investigation, positioning students to engage within the disciplines and come to understand for themselves the natural integration across all disciplines.

## QUESTIONS FOR REFLECTION

1. What are ways that literacy learning clubs may support students' learning within the special areas described in this chapter and/or areas not discussed? What are the opportunities and challenges?

2. Consider your own curriculums within these disciplines. How can this approach inform students' learning?

3. What do you hope students leave the class understanding about the discipline? How can the literacy learning clubs paradigm support this goal?

4. The examples presented in this chapter "spill over" into other classes. Are there places where you might consider collaborating with a colleague from another discipline to implement literacy learning clubs? What needs to be in place for this collaboration to be productive?

## ACTIVITIES TO CONSIDER

Consider the recommendations outlined in this chapter. As you consider the idea of literacy learning clubs within the special areas, do you see opportunities for collaboration? Consider collaborating with a colleague from another area to identify points of intersection across curricula to potentially develop a unit of study that integrates the literacy learning club paradigm. After completion, consider:

- What did students learn as they began this task?
- How did engaging with the curriculum using the literacy learning club model influence students' understanding of the content?
- How would you integrate this paradigm in the future?

## PART III

# LITERACY LEARNING CLUBS OUTSIDE THE CLASSROOM

## CHAPTER 9

# Literacy Learning Clubs
# for Civic Engagement

In this chapter, I step inside literacy learning clubs as a tool for supporting civic engagement. This chapter is intentionally placed near the end of the text, a culminating chapter of sorts, because it blends the disciplinary literacy work described in the previous chapters in ways that look outward toward the community instead of inward toward the school and classroom. In this chapter, literacy learning clubs are seen to offer a bridge across disciplines and into the community, further blending the boundaries of classroom space and academic disciplines in transformative ways. Recent work with children and adolescents has been looking at civic engagement through the lens of social justice, illustrating that examining beliefs about human rights locally, nationally, and internationally connects people with their community and about the shared responsibility of being part of a democratic society (Dunkerly & Bean, 2014).

In the previous chapters, I investigated how the paradigm of literacy learning clubs maps onto the traditional school structure that is organized around disciplines and special areas. In some ways, this is an artificial use of what is meant to be an authentic examination of learning through literacy, but it is necessary given that we must help students develop within these content areas and it is the way most schools are currently structured. In this chapter, we blend the boundaries of the typical school schedule and consider how literacy learning clubs can be a transformative way to honor the demands of curriculum and standards through alternative frameworks that have the potential to create partnerships across disciplines, grade levels, schools, communities, and national and international initiatives. Literacy learning clubs can be catalysts for helping developing adolescents understand their role within the larger community in which they live.

Opportunity exists as well to step outside of the disciplinary boundaries and use literacy learning clubs as a vehicle for helping students become active participants in the community at all levels, including classroom, school, local, national, and international engagement. In doing so, the focus is not on a single discipline but on the natural integration of multiple disciplines and the literacy lenses used within each to solve real-world problems. This natural integration is discussed with examples in previous chapters. In this chapter, we step outside specific disciplines and standards and instead use the world around the students, at whatever capacity they are ready to connect, to demonstrate how this paradigm becomes a catalyst for helping youth and adolescents understand their power to effect change. It can become a powerful tool for developing a voice.

The examples presented are designed to support elementary school teachers who are responsible for multiple subjects as well as those teachers who are content specialists and teach the same subject for multiple periods throughout the day. This chapter describes how literacy learning clubs can motivate students to recognize literacy as a means for social change as classrooms become blended with a sense of the local and global community in which students and teachers are positioned. The International Literacy Association (formerly the International Reading Association) states this position in *Adolescent Literacy* (Position Statement): "Multimodal literacy events allow students to comprehend and compose in and through print and nonprint text while also becoming an avenue for adolescents to link to the larger world in which they live" (2012, p. 10). Civic engagement in our schools today can be about inspiring what is popularly referred to as "social justice," and literacy learning clubs can be used as a framework to inspire these opportunities for children.

## What Does It Mean to Be "Civically Engaged"?

Civics has generally been defined as helping students recognize the role they play within the political structure of their community. Civics has a long history in American education, having been added to the school curriculum with the intent of helping students understand democracy and their role within that democracy. Earlier versions of civics in schools have been criticized as offering a one-dimensional view of being an engaged citizen. One perspective is that some of the policies and practices that are part of public school education in the United States such as the Pledge of Allegiance and the debate over prayer in schools, among others, offer a singular perspective of what it means to be a citizen. There is a belief by some in the educational community that civics education, which has traditionally been linked to social studies, is "lost" and "needed" in order for children to understand their role in the community in which they live.

Those who reject the more traditional views of civics education do not oppose the inclusion of community-oriented experiences but instead suggest that we need an ideological shift about what civics education means for student learning. Civics education is not, for example, just about students learning the processes of living in a democratic society but also about considering their relationship to their local, national, and international community. It is about creating opportunities for students to see how their beliefs can inform their actions and have an impact. It is also about helping students recognize how they can have a relationship with cultures and communities outside of their own.

This evolving definition suggests that civic engagement should be about helping children understand their role within the global community. Dunkerly and Bean (2014) offer this description: "Whereas traditional definitions of civic engagement have historically been tied to a particular locale or nation-state, we now have the opportunity through digital means to facilitate learning experiences that address both local and global conditions through human rights education and civic engagement" (p. 3). This dialogic view of civic engagement reflects an ideological shift suggesting that to be an engaged citizen is to move beyond understanding and to participate in specific democratic processes and practices, attaining a more nuanced view of the power of the individual to shape established norms.

This *cosmopolitanism,* which has a long history of addressing diverse perspectives, is emerging as a way of understanding youth and adolescent literacy development and engaging them in learning experiences (Harper, Bean, & Dunkerly, 2010). Current perspectives on civic engagement suggest that it is about impact and not assimilation and that it has evolved recently to become a conversation about *social justice.* But what actually is meant by notions of social justice? From the perspective of the literacy learning club, it offers a direct path for developing adolescents to use literacy in real ways to engage in the world around them by connecting with relevant issues (Duke, 2014; Lima & Oakes, 2013).

This type of civic engagement is often rooted in community initiatives. These initiatives are often found in after-school programs and community-based opportunities to engage in work designed to "make a difference." The list of what these activities encompass is long. Examples include working in a local soup kitchen, organizing supply drives, and developing partnerships with people in the community in need of some type of support. These types of initiatives have often been relegated to the work of Boy or Girl Scout projects, faith- and/or community-based projects, or after-school clubs. The focal point, of course, is the act of contributing to the community in meaningful ways that suggest our *engagement* with others is a necessary part of living in a community. A recent program, *Junior InVision*, organized through a local YMCA, is just one example of many of this type that is offered for upper elementary and middle school students as a way to connect to the community (see Figure 9.1).

Programs such as these can and do offer significant opportunities for students to become involved in the community, but being separated from curricula and the school day, they send the message that they are not academic programs. These programs, however, do provide the opportunity for people to use their academic expertise for organizational purposes. Working at the local soup kitchen, for example, may require the ability to organize supplies and ingredients (math) while also advertising the opportunity through multiple outlets (literacy). Literacy learning clubs bring this into the classroom in a way that engages students in authentic problem solving. They require that students draw on the multiple disciplinary skills explored in Chapters 5–8 in ways that are so embedded in the lives they lead and the work they do that participants may not even realize all of the skills they are drawing on to achieve success (Duke, 2014; Lima & Oakes, 2013). These exemplars offer an authentic experience that positions youth and adolescents to become college and career ready.

These opportunities for youth and adolescents have often been relegated to community experiences or clubs. What if they were brought into the classroom and the academic skills were taught in relation to the authentic problems the students were trying to solve? This is the goal of literacy learning clubs as a pathway to developing this evolving descriptor of civic engagement. It is a not a *choice* between attending to the curriculum and standards *or* engaging in these action- and advocacy-oriented experiences. By engaging in these experiences, children understand the benchmarks outlined in standards and curriculums in the ways that the goal of preparing students for career and adult readiness intended.

As explored in previous chapters, schools that organize academic content according to discipline are creating artificial boundaries. For example, children

---

Good for Others, Good for You

Participating in the Junior InVision program gives you the chance to activate your social responsibility by helping our neighbors receive the support they need to feel healthy, connected and secure.

---

**FIGURE 9.1.** Central New Jersey YMCA announcement (2016). Volunteer opportunities and ideas can be found at *www.ymca.net/volunteer/*.

and adolescents do not grow up using math in isolation from literacy and social studies. Instead, our daily lives are a natural integration, for both professional and personal purposes, of all these skills in order to accomplish individual, social, and professional goals. Bringing real-world issues into the classroom—either those that are classroom or school based or those that impact the local community or even state, national, and international issues—invites the opportunity to address that integration in a mediated environment. Quite simply, it helps children see how their expertise can matter and make a difference. What is more engaging and worthwhile than that? Suddenly, the need to be more literate or to use computational skills accurately takes on greater importance once it is removed from an abstract assignment and linked to a serious problem that needs solving. That is, it becomes real.

## How Have Students Demonstrated Civic Engagement?

The terms used to describe this type of experience range from "authentic learning" to "project-based learning" to "integrated curriculum," and so on. While it would be an oversimplification to suggest they all mean exactly the same thing, what connects these terms is the notion that students learn best when it is purposeful. Few argue with this concept, and yet recent trends in education suggest that such activities are relegated to the fringes or to the academically elite and are rarely seen as the heart of instruction. A strong research base suggests that when this approach is at the heart of learning, then curricular expertise across the content areas strengthens.

Nell Duke (2014) offers this paradigm of learning for educators to consider:

> In a project-based approach, students work over an extended time period for a purpose beyond satisfying a school requirement—to build something, to create something, to respond to a question they have, to solve a real problem, or to address a real need. . . . Along the way, teachers build knowledge and teach skills, but in the students' mind, the knowledge and skills serve to meet the project's goal (while in the teacher's mind they may also serve to address specific state standards, meet district curriculum requirements, and so on). (p. 11)

It is this difference in goals that allows learning to feel natural and educators to satisfy the range of curricular and external requirements needed for students to progress. Currently, this is being described as integrating social justice into the curriculum. The terminology is not as significant as the goals. Literacy learning clubs offer a paradigm to make this a central piece of classroom instruction, though the same paradigm has been demonstrated to be successful in after-school experiences as well (Casey, 2012a, 2012b).

Several years ago I worked with children in a low-income neighborhood in a community-based after-school program. It was my first time working with the idea of literacy learning clubs, and I initially found greater acceptance in the after-school program than the local school because there was not the pressure of standards and established curriculum. There was a "what do we have to lose?" feeling about piloting this work, and gratitude was expressed that I was willing to run a program for free.

I worked with the staff and the children to identify topics that were of interest to students in grades 4–8 who attended the program. Once these students were identified, the teachers and I were able to secure donations from local organizations and two national publishing outlets to provide them with the research material to create a synthesis of their learning. We had limited availability to computers as well. Topics ranged from music history to animals, theater, and so forth and culminated with a community presentation of their findings. Throughout, students drew on multiple disciplines, digital tools, and traditional print-based work to build knowledge and became empowered to dive into this work after school because they had *choice* throughout our month together (Casey, 2012b). This same lens can move from individual interest to community concerns and in my later work with teachers was integrated into the school day effectively (Casey, 2012a).

Dunkerly and Bean (2014) describe how adolescents' natural reactions to national events (in their example, immigration policy and reform) provided the catalyst for linking to literacy learning and development.

> "That's not fair!" "They can't do that!" "Where are they going to go?" Such were the responses from a class of middle school students after learning that despite the existence of human rights that guarantee asylum and the right of nationality to all people, countries can still block refugees and immigrants fleeing oppression, violence, and poverty. In response, the students at Arroyo International Charter School (pseudonym) drew from their readings of global young adult literature and human rights simulations, as well as their own experiences, to create a short film that took to task the treatment of immigrants and refugees both locally and globally. (p. 1)

In Dunkerly and Bean's work, students, inspired by their frustration, draw on multiple print and nonprint resources that reflect a range of genres to develop a short film that ultimately served as a public service announcement to outline their beliefs about what is needed for immigration reform. As the group problem solves, debates, and researches, teachers are facilitating and modeling the multiple literacy skills across a variety of disciplines needed to navigate and synthesize the range of materials students actively seek out because they are seen as avenues for understanding an identified concern, in this case, immigration reform.

There is no shortage of "objectives" and "standards" that are infused in this work. The shift is that it is not the objective or standard dictating the students' literacy learning experiences. Instead, the students' need to solve a perceived problem leads the learning, and the standards and objectives get woven in accordingly. This is not as neat a model as a scripted curriculum that carefully and linearly "checks off" the required boxes as outlined by standards and curricular benchmarks, but it is arguably more effective. This model trusts the educators involved to make good decisions about linking the necessary learning experiences to students' natural inquiry.

As I write this text, we are in the midst of a presidential election. The National Writing Project has developed a resource to empower student voice and engage student writers by bringing them into the national debate (see Figure 9.2).

*Letters to the Next President* is infused with opportunities to read and write in a variety of genres, with technology embedded in ways that clearly align with what is called for in the CCSS. The focus for the adolescent participants, however, is on engaging in real debate about issues that matter to them in powerful ways. The standards and curriculum content are evident and can be documented by educators, but the students are most interested in having their voice heard in the absence of the right to vote.

---

HOW L2P 2.0 WORKS

L2P 2.0 starts by supporting you—the teachers and mentors thinking about how to engage their students in the coming election. Throughout the spring and summer of 2016, L2P 2.0 will gather a wide range of partners to provide resources, host live conversations, and point to technology tools that you can use with the young people you work with. The L2P 2.0 monthly bulletins, as well as the Letters to the Next President 2.0 website, are your guide to what is coming up. You are encouraged to participate in as much or as little as you would like, and we welcome your contributions to the community discussions on social media. You'll find them through the hashtag #2nextprez.

In late July, L2P 2.0 will launch the Letters to the Next President showcase site where young people (13–18) will be invited to publish their writing or multimedia work with readers from around the country. This site will be open for publication by youth up until election day, and will remain open to promote and highlight youth voice and work into the inaugural year.

We're excited to have you on board!

---

**FIGURE 9.2.** National Writing Project *Letters to the Next President* (2016). See *http://letters 2president.org/* for complete information.

# How Can Literacy Learning Clubs Become a Paradigm for Civic Engagement?

The literacy learning club framework that positions individual learning through social collaboration is a natural framework for civic engagement. The work of Duke, Dunkerly, and Bean, together with my own research, documents children, tweens, and teens working collaboratively to engage in action-oriented projects. This can span from working to create an optimal learning space in the classroom to working to develop a clothes/food drive for a local shelter to developing persuasive print and nonprint text about national and international environmental practices that students oppose. None of these "projects" falls within a single discipline but instead requires the integration of multiple disciplinary literacy skills to engage in the work. In doing so, students are building multiple discrete literacy skills and content area skills. These can grow and become school-based initiatives that invite students to work across grade levels. In the sections that follow, we step into two school-based exemplars.

## Literacy Learning Clubs in Practice: Voices from the Classroom

### Moss School

Lima and Oakes (2013) describe service learning as an opportunity to build social awareness for students studying biology and engineering. In doing so, they have created the "playground project" that aims to support the local community in which their university is situated by partnering the university students studying these fields with local elementary schools in need of safe and engaging play spaces. Lima and Oakes have studied this primarily through their work with their own university students engaged in their own service learning. Another perspective is to consider how the elementary students' involvement in a project such as this one helps students to learn a variety of academic skills by becoming engaged in this community need.

Let's consider an idea such as this one from the children's perspective.

The children, educators, and parents of Moss School, a grade K–8 elementary school, are voicing frustration over the lack of a safe play space for the children. Moss School has recently invested a significant amount of resources in digital tools to support learning but spent little to no money on the deteriorating playground that has become so unsafe that sections of the large area of land are not available for play. This year, the principal, Ms. H, read about the work being done in Louisiana and wonders if she can re-create a similar type of project within her own community.

In a school-level meeting, Ms. H speaks about the possibility and the teachers are on board to take it to the students. Ms. H is clear, however, that owing to the low test scores the school has been battling this cannot be a departure from academic learning. While some of the faculty are not interested in what they describe as "more work," a core group of teachers across the grade levels are excited about the possibility of engaging their students in a project that may positively impact their own community. As a result of this enthusiastic support, a committee made up of grade-level representatives from grades 1–8 is formed to build the project, and "Let's Play at Moss" is born. Before they begin, each teacher involved in the project communicates with his or her class of students what is being proposed and the students are enthusiastic about contributing.

The upper grade/middle school team (grades 4–8) representatives decide that they will take the lead on the project because the skills needed (math, literacy, and technology) link well with the curricular demands in those grade levels. The school decides to organize groups according to interest in the piece of the project, so 2 hours a week are set aside for all teachers/students participating to work with their cross grade-level peers. The initial areas of responsibility include:

- Determine the focus of responsibilities.
- Develop and analyze a schoolwide survey about playground needs.
- Create a scale of available space.
- Put together models for consideration.
- Create a grant proposal to fund the project.

While each cross grade-level cluster has a primary area of responsibility, they all work together and share across classes through classroom visits and collaborations. The teachers and students quickly learn of the constant need for collaboration as the project is a series of moving parts.

The teachers select areas of focus based on content within the curriculum, and while it seems to fall primarily within math and literacy to do the necessary research to develop the surveys, create scales and models, as well as locate and develop grant proposals, they quickly learn that the students need to pull in history, geography, and science as they consider the viability of the land and space among other challenges to make decisions. In addition, they also quickly learn the need to pull in community advocates and experts who both help streamline the funding process and provide the necessary expertise to understand what works and does not work in the identified play space.

In this imagined project, there is much to do and many mistakes to learn from as students work together to solve this schoolwide problem. Students initially survey the other students in the building about what they would like to see in a new playground and a "wish list" is developed. When the team of students who created the survey review the findings, they realize that not everything can be realistically accomplished, given what they are learning about the space, funding, and feasibility of the project. They revise accordingly. The scale models are understood by some, but not all, so teachers reteach small groups how to scale space, and they use students who have a strong understanding of the concept to share their work. The grant proposals require a careful reading of the directions and a strong understanding of how to synthesize the data collected as well as a study of the genre itself. Building models requires a study of rudimentary engineering and design, and so on. The cross grade levels are tricky because of differing developmental needs. One of the teachers compares it to a developing adolescent Montessori approach. However, the motivation around the topic as well as the opportunity for choice alleviates much of this frustration for students and teachers as they seek out new paradigms for teaching and learning.

The literacy learning club framework becomes the organizing tool that the teachers and students turn to when they are ready to move this work forward. Most teachers devote 1 to 2 days of the week from September to February to develop the project, and then they coordinate dates as needed as construction begins. Scheduling is hard and does not always happen in the way the teachers and students would like. Benchmarks and high-stakes testing need to be attended to, as do curricular requirements that are not part of this experience.

A teacher/facilitator supports each of the groups. When they gather, as outlined in Chapter 3, they begin with a focusing session on the topic, move to a gathering of resources, the group collaboration in the club time, and then the focusing finish where they log on their individual digital blog what was accomplished and what they are looking forward to next time. The session always concludes with a think-aloud where the teacher/facilitator gives voice to the literacy expertise needed to navigate a sample resource (using a diagram, reading a document about building playgrounds, among others) to model how to use the resources needed for the project.

The school has adopted a digital platform to organize this work. The students are working within Google Classroom, which streamlines interaction when face-to-face meetings are not possible. Google Classroom also gives students the opportunity to keep in constant communication with the other groups who are not expert in their area, so they can coordinate for the final project. The teachers had initially decided not to create a hierarchy of team captains, but a natural hierarchy developed, primarily around grade level, as older students facilitated and supported their younger colleagues.

Work that grew out of this experience included a short video developed and narrated by the students to accompany the grant proposal; it documented what the students believed was a clear need. A team of students also presented their findings from the survey and their recommendations to the Board of Education as part of the process of being transparent about the work that was being done. Presentations, videos, and writing in different genres have long been part of what counts as "school," but when it is used for a real purpose suddenly students are invested in ways that the seemingly abstract literacy experiences that only exist in the school space resist.

Much as in the real world, projects such as these are messy and at times frustrating, but overall they are very satisfying and worthwhile. Students are eager to understand the content of the mini-lessons and the concepts underscored by the curriculum and standards because that knowledge offers the tools they need to complete the project. The learning is not an end but a means through which they can successfully advocate for something that matters to them. It is not about learning scale to complete a worksheet, or writing an imaginary proposal, or creating a survey that will go nowhere. In doing so, the learning becomes powerful and meaningful, and all involved learn that their academic expertise and experiences are needed in order to participate in change that has an immediate effect on their own school community.

The example of this schoolwide effort may seem overwhelming to those who are considering adopting this structure in the school. The value of literacy learning clubs as a vehicle for civic engagement is the opportunity they afford to scale up or down based on the demands of the project.

## Johnson Middle School

In another example, in Johnson Middle School, in an urban environment a seventh-grade social studies class is learning about the presidential race. They are hearing about issues that are new to them, such as immigration, budget, and even education, and are having a difficult time finding the facts amidst all the rhetoric. Ms. M decides this is the perfect moment to dive into some relevant issues. She creates a spreadsheet on the conversations they have been listening to, and, together, the class creates a list of "hot topics" in the election. They identify

- Budget
- Safety and security
- Education
- Environment

Students then select a group that they are most interested in understanding more about. The class has constructed a website titled "Minding our business . . . Ms. M's class dives into the election." Each group has a page on the site and is charged with developing resources as well as a short informational video clip about their topic.

Ms. M allots 2 weeks of study for this project and follows the literacy learning framework for each 40-minute class. This includes the focusing session, the club gathering time, the club meeting, and the focusing finish. Each session concludes with her modeling her own thinking as she shares a newspaper excerpt, a piece of a debate, and even political advertisements actively demonstrating how she reads each of these texts to arrive at her own conclusions. Ms. M also uses the digital platforms that have been identified as so helpful (though not essential) to this work. The development of a website allows for an audience as well as participation from others around the school and within the community. The use of Edmodo creates a space where students can work on the task at hand collaboratively both synchronously and asynchronously.

Over the course of their work, the students investigate rhetoric, use of persuasive messaging, and genre, delve into the history of elections, and explore complex mathematics as they search to understand the delegate process as compared to the popular vote. In this scenario, civic engagement is about raising awareness of the multiple tools used when developing messages, as well as how to sift through multiple media to identify information and locate sources for corroboration. It is a sophisticated endeavor that Ms. M recognizes many adults struggle with, which is why it is important, she believes, to introduce as students are developing as adolescents.

## Summary

Current trends in civics education are shifting from a study of students' role in their own community to an awareness of the role they play in the global community and the power of advocacy and action to support change. This shift in civic engagement is often used interchangeably with empowering a sense of social justice among adolescents. Literacy learning clubs offer a pathway for developing an awareness of civic engagement in developing adolescents. It empowers students to work collaboratively to solve problems they care about, using cross-disciplinary literacy throughout. The teacher works to explain the types of discipline-specific literacies students need to engage in the work. This forum is a natural blending of academic disciplines and disciplinary literacy and bridges the classroom to the community in ways that are potentially transformative for learning.

## QUESTIONS FOR REFLECTION

1. What possibilities for civic engagement exist in your curricular unit of study? Consider the classroom and schoolwide level. Are there opportunities for integration?

2. What opportunities are available for community partnerships?

3. What explicit academic skills are needed to accomplish these partnerships?

## ACTIVITIES TO CONSIDER

Survey students in your class, grade level, or school about issues that are of concern to them. Use the survey results to collaborate with colleagues to create a literacy learning club paradigm that invites students to become active participants in this issue. Throughout, document how you are meeting curricular goals and objectives when the learning is driven by this larger community initiative. At the conclusion of the experience, consider:

- What did you notice about student engagement in this experience?

- What types of discipline-specific literacy practices did students draw from in order to participate in this project?

- What curricular goals and objectives were met? How did meeting these objectives differ from traditional lessons designed to support these curricular objectives?

- How might you implement these in the future? What pieces of your pilot would you retain, and what would you change?

## CHAPTER 10

# Literacy Learning Clubs to Support Schoolwide Literacy Efforts

In the previous chapters, we examined how literacy learning clubs support students in their development of disciplinary literacy as a pathway for understanding academic content. In this chapter, we consider how this paradigm can be a support for educators' professional development within a department, school, or district. As educators across disciplines begin to consider the disciplinary literacy lenses students use in their classes as well as the value of collaborative inquiry across the school day, a similar paradigm can be used for adult learning and professional development.

Following are suggestions for bringing these ideas into your schools for professional development purposes. Much as we began the journey together with the request that you read these words with your own students' needs and context in mind, I ask the same as you consider your own professional context and the way these recommendations may be adapted to best suit your professional growth and the growth of your colleagues.

## How Can Literacy Learning Clubs Be Used for Professional Development Purposes?

Research on professional development *that works* in school districts is similar, in many ways, to the work of literacy learning clubs themselves. To begin this journey in your own grade level or school, it is important to distinguish between *professional training* and *professional development*. The typical model of professional development in school districts often follows the training model. Teachers gather together for a short period of time (usually for a day or an after-school meeting or two) to receive information about a new program, initiative, and standards—often because they have been "volun-told," a favorite term used by a principal I often work with. These days can be quite engaging as teachers work to develop activities and strategies to introduce to students. It may even inspire teachers to try things with their students. The model is neat and often affordable. It is not, however, sustainable, as the resulting shifts in teacher practice are surface level because educators have not been given the time necessary to delve into this new knowledge in ways that allow them to consider how it might influence their own beliefs about teaching and learning.

Our discussion in this chapter parallels the discussion in earlier chapters of the difference between memorizing a particular formula in mathematics and using the formula in relevant, purposeful ways that allow students to understand its utility. Memorizing may allow for success on the test or task; using empowers students to use this learning in multiple contexts independent of the classroom or teacher. The strategy that is useful may be used once or twice, but if it is not anchored to the educators' beliefs about learning, it will either be forgotten or will not be adapted in ways that may have been more useful (Bean, 2015).

The training model may shift some practices, but it falls short in helping teachers shape their belief systems. When learning a new grading program, a new school procedure, or even about new resources, the training model may be quite appropriate. Where this model fails, however, is in supporting teachers in ways that motivate sustained change in beliefs about student learning (Bean, 2015). It may inspire some to continue to learn about a topic introduced, but that connection is haphazard and unpredictable, at best, and, at worst, becomes a waste of valuable time as teachers leave their learning at the workshop door. In order for teachers and schools to integrate the literacy learning club paradigm as well as other focused professional shifts into their work, thoughtful integration must take place. That approach takes time and resources (Casey, Kawalek, Young, & Harris, 2016).

*Professional development* refers to the opportunity to engage in formal and informal learning experiences that will motivate participants to integrate new ideas and practices into their existing paradigms. True professional development looks beyond shifts in practice to examine ways for teachers to begin questioning their own beliefs (Casey et al., 2016; Mickler & Irvin, 2015). Cursory shifts in practice often result in short-term shifts that are not deeply connected to beliefs about children's learning and development. Examining practices in ways that give participants time to consider how children learn offers more opportunity for impacting belief systems in transformative ways (Bean, 2015).

Professional development models that motivate sustained change interrogate professional practice using a variety of strategies (Casey et al., 2016; Ippolito, Dobbs, Charner-Laird, & Lawrence, 2016). This is inclusive of some whole-group sessions designed to introduce an initiative and small-group professional learning communities organized around either teacher interest (preferred) or district needs (often necessary), where a common topic or text unites small groups, allowing them to have extended conversation over several sessions, sometimes over an academic year, with the classroom becoming a laboratory where ideas are tried.

For example, if the present text were to become part of a PLC, groups could choose to cycle through each chapter in a linear fashion and "try on" the strategies suggested between meetings to debrief and discover what works or does not work in the teachers' settings. Similarly, some might choose to study specific sections of the text, depending on the teaching assignment.

Compare the potential learning if you were to be given the time to absorb the material presented in this text over an extended period of time in ways that would lead you to adapt the proposed methods and ideas to your unique context. Imagine reading sections that matter to your work with colleagues who have a shared interest. Couple that with time allotted either virtually or in person to talk with others about portions that seem to fit and that you plan to implement and then try these ideas out, knowing that you will return to these safe conversations to debrief, deconstruct, and reconstruct beliefs about teaching and learning. Consider, for a moment, the training model. Imagine if the content in this text were delivered as a single-session workshop, with the expectation that you would begin implementation with little to no followthrough or support. Both opportunities introduce educators to the literacy learning club framework. The first does so in a way that aligns with research on adult learning. The second focuses on transmitting information, with little attention given to audience participation and understanding. Research on professional development suggests that the training scenario will result in short-term shifts in practice and has greater potential for misuse or misunderstanding when implementation occurs (Lieberman & Miller, 2014).

Just as the students in the discipline-specific chapters (Chapters 5–8) and the focus on civic engagement (Chapter 9) used digital platforms to maintain synchronous and asynchronous conversation outside of the classroom time, so too can this be a successful venue for professional development. It may be organized by grade level or discipline and can happen according to contractual meeting schedules, or it may be more organic and develop in response to topics teachers want to pursue further. For example, one of the schools I frequent has developed "Tech Share Tuesday," and using a Google Document, teachers can sign up to share a new tool or technique they have identified. All professionals in the school community have access to that information, and if it is of interest they gather in the teacher's classroom to learn more about it. At the heart of the success are the *choice, collaboration,* and *organization* that unite the experience. The follow-up is informal and may occur in the hallway, e-mails, and planned meetings.

Just as successful, though a more formal application, is the example of a school district moving to adopt professional learning communities as their primary vehicle for professional development. In this example, the administrators develop topics based on analysis of formative and summative assessment data, and each grade level forms groups to investigate the areas of concern. For example, in one fifth-grade classroom, the group may be studying reading non-narrative text; in another, it may be using conferencing in the workshop model. A leader of each group—sometimes an informal teacher leader in the building and other times an administrator—is identified, and the groups meet once a month during a contractually scheduled time to review key professional texts and resources. At the conclusion of each session, everyone leaves with a strategy or resource to try in the classroom and report back. In addition, within each group there is at least one other grade-level or discipline-area colleague who acts as an informal liaison on the day-to-day hallway talk of teaching. They are bound together by topic, not text, but similar to what we saw with the students engaged in the literacy learning clubs, they often use professional texts and resources to learn more about the topic. The use of digital resources can unite the school as teachers gather and post resources for their own professional learning community; others in the building or district have access to the discussion boards and resource posts for their own work.

At the conclusion of a session of study, the teams of teachers share their resources with an informal workshop at a department or grade-level meeting, where these resources are contextualized for everyone and all of the teacher participants can engage in professional leadership. This approach allows the participants to question the experiences and also gives them time to adapt in ways appropriate for their contexts. In addition, because the participants are engaged throughout, their work as professionals is heightened as they work to integrate the new knowledge in ways that will help their own practice and their students' learning. This process creates a sense of professional identity that is absent in those who passively participate in school-mandated training sessions. Developing a professional identity is a critical aspect of creating a culture of learning in schools (ILA, 2016; Lieberman & Miller, 2014; Mickler & Irvin, 2015).

Making this sustained professional development even more effective are those schools that have coaches available to model lessons and offer feedback as teachers try new initiatives. It is critical that the person assigned to this role not be seen as an evaluator but instead as a contributor. Central to the success of all of these models is the use of collaboration to support individual study (Bean, 2015). Just as the theory and research explored in Chapters 1 and 2 suggest that learning is social and that social collaboration deepens individual understanding, so too does this lens help shape this perspective of professional development. As you begin to review professional development models for integrating literacy learning clubs into your classroom, or program, consider:

- The organization (grade level, discipline level, school study).
- How these can be incorporated (around a topic of study, a question that crosses disciplines, etc.).
- Methods for organization (what part of the school day this can happen, whether digital collaborations are possible, etc.).

## Building Bridges: Looking Outside the School Community to Engage in Literacy Learning Clubs for Literacy Advocacy

We can look outside the school for the use of these learning communities as well. Recent work such as the ILA (2016) *Frameworks for Literacy Education Reform* is designed to create opportunities for those not directly involved in K–12 education (i.e., those responsible for policy as well as parents), who remain on the fringe of the educational community and yet are fully invested and at times holding more power than the educators themselves.

Publications designed to educate the community on preferred practices in literacy education may be transformative if they are studied using the literacy learning club model. Consider texts written for the noneducator shepherding children through the complexity of changes and standards in a way designed to inform parents (e.g., ILA, 2016; Walsh, 2016). Study of these texts and others like it through virtual and face-to-face school-based parent groups could be powerful in educating parents about literacy research and practice and could also inform community members who do not typically have a voice in educational decisions. It provides an avenue for creating communities that advocate for children. Beginning with questions from the community and using these topics to drive the club meetings with texts, such as those cited and others drawn in as needed, can help create informed communities that may make a difference in student learning.

The ILA's (2016) Literacy Reform Task Force white paper distills key research on children's literacy learning in a narrative intended for those who influence policy. The goal is to create dialogue with those outside of education to support what the authors of the document identify as preferred practice. Publications and conversations that target audiences outside of education offer an opportunity to build community bridges. Use of the literacy learning club both for K–12 professional development and for creating community conversations has great potential. It gives voice to a range of perspectives within the community in a way that supports deep investigation instead of a surface, cursory review.

At the heart of the literacy learning club, whether found in a fifth-grade classroom, a schoolwide civic activity, a professional development experience, or as an opportunity for community study, is the belief that learning is social. If we are to empower children to be expert readers, writers, and thinkers in the disciplines; if we are to support teachers as professionals with evolving belief systems that are far more complex than the technician model we often ask them to wear; and if we expect our community partners to be vested in preferred practices for children, then we need to consider paradigms that support learning and learners that value the expertise of all involved. This paradigm is born of the research on motivation and engagement that suggests choice as essential for engaging all learners, children and adult; it is located in the belief that learning is not a collection of discrete skills but rather the nuanced understanding of how academic expertise translates into the ability to successfully navigate the world in which we live. It requires time to work with others to understand perspective as well as seize the opportunity for individual integration in order to build a schema of knowledge.

We began our study of literacy learning clubs in Chapter 1 with Frank Smith's (1987) invitation to join the literacy club. The world is shifting and shaping print and nonprint text in ways that we have yet to imagine. To stay current with these shifts, we need to move beyond learning as a collection of information and instead engage in paradigms that motivate thinking and understanding, "knowing and ways of knowing." It is important for the educational community to look beyond singular strategies and resources and seek comprehensive paradigms that invite participants to understand how literacy is shaped by the demands of the text and task that are inclusive of traditional print materials as well as digital literacies. It requires that we have a deep respect and trust for children and adolescents and for the educators who work with them so that they can be empowered to make decisions to create these deep learning experiences—experiences described throughout this text and already happening in many classrooms. I invite you to consider the literacy learning club as a paradigm for your work in the ways that matter for you, your students, your colleagues, and your community.

## Summary

Just as literacy learning clubs offer a framework for deep learning across the disciplines, so too can they be a tool for supporting sustained professional development in the schools. Research on professional development acknowledges the need for extended study of new initiatives, whether mandated or self-selected, using a variety of methods. These include workshop training models as needed, time for collaborative conversation with colleagues, coaching support, and opportunity for piloting new ideas, materials, and practices in the classroom, preferably with coaching support and time to discuss findings with colleagues. This extended study is more challenging to schedule, but the results are more permanent.

Adopting this extended approach to professional development also allows educators to build a professional identity in ways that passive training models do not.

The framework of the literacy learning clubs maps onto this forum for professional development effectively and is inclusive of all the components necessary for deep learning. This framework can be adopted for the study of this text and the ideas within it, or it can be used to implement initiatives outside of the scope of this work. The structure is consistent in its ability to support professional development because at its core is the flexibility necessary for educators to adapt to support the professional learning goals. Literacy learning clubs for adolescents and the adults who work with them honor the expertise of all involved and rely on professional judgment throughout implementation.

## QUESTIONS FOR REFLECTION

1. How do you envision using the literacy learning club for your work?

2. What types of professional development experiences are available in your context that may support this integration?

3. How can the literacy learning club framework support professional development goals aside from those described in this chapter? Is there a place for this framework for initiatives that fall outside of the study of disciplinary literacy as discussed throughout the text?

## ACTIVITIES TO CONSIDER

- If several colleagues are interested in the content of this book, use this book as an anchor for your own professional learning club. As you make plans for using this text to engage in your own professional learning club around integrating literacy learning clubs, consider the following:
  - What is the goal of this study?
  - How many meeting sessions are you considering?

- Will these be face to face, or will they be conducted virtually?
- Will you use a digital platform to stay connected? How?
- How will you organize your reading (chapter by chapter, selected chapters, etc.)?

Consider professional learning initiatives that you are interested in pursuing or that the district is dictating. How can the literacy learning club paradigm as explored in this chapter be a useful model for investigating these areas of professional inquiry? As you answer this question, consider:

- What is the goal of this study?
- How many meeting sessions are you considering?
- Will these be face to face, or will they be conducted virtually?
- Will you use a digital platform to stay connected? How?
- What is the culminating product you plan to develop (a unit, curriculum revision, assessment tools, etc.)?

- Literacy learning clubs as a tool for community conversations. Consider using the literacy learning club framework as a paradigm for engaging the community (parents, interested community members) in a deep conversation about the role of literacy in learning as well as in preparation for career readiness. Some texts that may be of interest for a community study include *A Parent's Guide to Public Education in the 21st Century: Navigating Education Reform to Get the Best Education for My Child* (Walsh, 2016) and *Frameworks for Literacy Education Reform* (ILA, 2016).

# APPENDIX

# SAMPLE PLANNING GUIDES, FORMS, AND RESOURCES

# Lesson Plan for Learning Clubs:
# Motivating Middle School Readers and Writers

| | |
|---|---|
| Grades: | 6–8 |
| Lesson plan type | Standard lesson |
| Estimated time | Six 45-minute sessions |
| Lesson Author | Heather Casey, Edison, New Jersey |
| | Suzanne Gespass, Lawrenceville, New Jersey |
| Publisher | International Reading Association |

## PREVIEW

### Overview

In this lesson, students participate in learning clubs, a grouping system used to organize active learning events based on student-selected areas of interest. Guided by the teacher, students select content-area topics and draw on multiple texts—including websites, printed material, video, and music—to investigate their topics. Students then have the opportunity to share their learning using similar media, such as learning blogs.

### From Theory to Practice

Casey, H. K. (2008). Engaging the disengaged: Using learning clubs to support struggling adolescent readers and writers. *Journal of Adolescent and Adult Literacy, 52*(4), 284–294.

- This article describes the use of learning clubs to motivate struggling students to engage in literacy events and foster literacy development.
- Effective teachers draw on the use of literature circles and book clubs to support learning across topics.
- The learning club structure motivates middle school students to draw on literacy as a tool for learning.
- Adolescents are engaging in multiple modes of texts outside of the classroom that have the potential to motivate learning within the classroom.

*(continued)*

Daniels, H. (2002). *Literature circles: Voice and choice in the student-centered classroom.* Portland, ME: Stenhouse.

- Students are motivated to read when given the opportunity to choose materials.
- Teachers retain control over the "menu" to select from as well as the formation of groups.
- Student-centered, constructivist group investigation around common texts necessitates the teacher carefully structure and organize the experience.

## STANDARDS

### NCTE/IRA National Standards for the English Language Arts

1. Students read a wide range of print and nonprint texts to build an understanding of texts, of themselves, and of the cultures of the United States and the world; to acquire new information; to respond to the needs and demands of society and the workplace; and for personal fulfillment. Among these texts are fiction and nonfiction, classic and contemporary works.

2. Students apply a wide range of strategies to comprehend, interpret, evaluate, and appreciate texts. They draw on their prior experience, their interactions with other readers and writers, their knowledge of word meaning and of other texts, their word identification strategies, and their understanding of textual features (e.g., sound–letter correspondence, sentence structure, context, graphics).

3. Students adjust their use of spoken, written, and visual language (e.g., conventions, style, vocabulary) to communicate effectively with a variety of audiences and for different purposes.

4. Students employ a wide range of strategies as they write and use different writing process elements appropriately to communicate with different audiences for a variety of purposes.

5. Students conduct research on issues and interests by generating ideas and questions, and by posing problems. They gather, evaluate, and synthesize data from a variety of sources (e.g., print and nonprint texts, artifacts, people) to communicate their discoveries in ways that suit their purpose and audience.

6. Students use a variety of technological and information resources (e.g., libraries, databases, computer networks, video) to gather and synthesize information and to create and communicate knowledge.

7. Students participate as knowledgeable, reflective, creative, and critical members of a variety of literacy communities.

8. Students use spoken, written, and visual language to accomplish their own purposes (e.g., for learning, enjoyment, persuasion, and the exchange of information).

*(continued)*

## RESOURCES AND PREPARATION

### Materials and Technology

- Computer with LCD projector capabilities for demonstration (optional but encouraged)
- Computers with Internet access (at least one per group)
- Blogger
- Magazines and books organized around topics of interest
- Learning log (folder with blank paper) as an alternative to blogs
- Paper and pencils/pens

### Printouts

- Open Interest Inventory
- Closed Interest Inventory
- Learning Clubs Rubric

### Websites

- IPL KidSpace
- 4Teachers.org
- KOL Homework Help
- CNN Student News
- Center for Media Literacy
- Field Trip Earth
- ALA: Great Web Sites for Kids
- History News Network
- Cobblestone and Cricket Publications

### Preparation

1. Hand out the Interest Inventories to survey students about areas of interest. Use the Open Interest Inventory to have students generate their own topics within a particular content area of unit of study; use the Closed Interest Inventory to limit the specific topics available for selection. Potential topics may include:
   - Science (e.g., gravity or motion)
   - Social studies cultural exploration (e.g., customs or children's hobbies in local, state, national, or international area of exploration)
   - Math (e.g., use of geometry in the workplace)

*(continued)*

- Health (e.g., age-appropriate exercises, food guides, or air quality)
- Alternatively, survey students about areas they are interested in learning more about and build groups based on the identified topics.

2. Form groups of no more than four students based on identified topics.

3. Create initial "learning tubs" with magazines and books organized around topics of interest for students to begin their investigations.

4. Bookmark applicable sites listed in the websites (and others you might find on particular topics) on your classroom computer or lab computers. If you do not have classroom computers with Internet access, reserve time in your school's computer lab for Session 2. If you plan on having your students blog, reserve time in your school's computer lab for all sessions.

5. If you plan on having your students blog, create a basic blog at Blogger to model for students in Session 1. Possible postings may include a picture, a brief description of what you (as a model student) are looking forward to learning, and potential links that may help the students once they begin.

6. If your students are unable to blog, make sure to provide a learning log (a folder with blank paper).

## INSTRUCTIONAL PLAN

### Student Objectives

Students will:

- Draw on literacy as a tool for learning by identifying multiple resources to support topics of investigation.
- Synthesize multiple types of texts and genres to gather information and support learning by working with varying modes of text and genres.
- Reflect on their roles as readers and writers across these texts through group conversation.
- Develop critical comprehension through investigations across texts
- Develop the ability to support individual and group learning goals by collaborating with peers in small-group settings

### Session 1: What Does It Mean to Use Literacy to Learn?

1. Discuss with students the characteristics of effective collaborations, such as listening to others, sharing ideas, and using conversation to encourage understanding. Model this by engaging with another student and/or colleague in a positive demonstration of effective listening and communicating. Also model a negative demonstration. Ask students to identify what worked and didn't work, and use that to begin building a list of how to support each other's learning in a group setting.

*(continued)*

148

2. Introduce students to learning clubs. Describe the role of learning clubs in the classroom. Explain that each learning club session will involve four steps. These include:

   - Class Meeting—a focused and short lesson to demonstrate using the materials to investigate learning.
   - Gathering Time—students locate information and work with their group to identify information around their topic.
   - Scribing Time—groups reflect in their learning logs or learning blogs about the content of the session as well as what supported and interfered with their learning. Groups using blogs to document and describe learning should switch the responsibility of the designated "scribe" at each session.
   - Group Meeting—members reflect on the session and establish goals for the next session. The group then discusses what they hope to achieve during the next session.

3. This session's Class Meeting is a procedural one. Use this time to help students build their learning blogs and/or learning logs which will support their inquiry and become a tool for sharing their learning with others. Model the sample blog you built. As you model the building of the blog, groups can follow along on their computers. At this point, students' blogs should include a framework for responses as well as their topic.

4. During Gathering Time, students should generate questions about their topic as well as potential resources. These resources may be web-based or print, such as books, magazines, and videos.

5. Have students respond to the question "What does it mean to use literacy to learn?" during Scribing Time. Possible guiding prompts include: "Review what you learned today. Has that learning been validated by multiple sources? If not, then think about where you can verify that information. What is left to learn? Write those items down in the form of a question to guide your work."

6. If time permits, students may upload some visuals to describe their investigations as well as questions they have about their selected topic of inquiry. They can do this as part of their Group Meeting.

### Session 2: Digital Literacies

1. Class meeting—Explain to students that the focus of today's class meeting is on using digital resources to support and demonstrate learning. Access a website that makes use of multiple media—including printed text and fixed and moving images—such as ALA: Great Web Sites for Kids. Using a think-aloud, demonstrate how to "read" these different texts to gather information. This is also an opportunity to model how to identify useful sources by identifying the author of the website. Potential questions to ask of students include:

   - "What do you think we trust more, information found on *National Geographic* or information discovered on a Facebook account?"
   - "How do we make decisions about whether or not what we read/see/hear is true?"

   *(continued)*

149

Consider modeling for students how web addresses can be deceiving. A potential web-site to explore is Museum of Hoaxes. This can invite conversations on how to be critical consumers of text we find on the Internet.

2. Gathering Time—Invite students to navigate the Internet using the sites you bookmarked to begin building their understanding of their topics.

   **Note:** Other sites may be added as the project continues. This should be encouraged and will shift depending on what students identify about their areas of interest. The sites provided in the websites list are broad and cover a range of topics typically found in middle school curriculums across the content areas.

3. Scribing Time—Ask students to gather into their groups to share information. You might say something like: "Now that you have had an opportunity to investigate independently, let's come together and talk about what we have learned. Begin by sharing what you have learned. As you listed to one another, think about how what you studied connects to what your group members studied. After you have finished sharing, think about how you are going to represent what you learned today. Are there pictures and video clips that can demonstrate what you learned? How will you write about your learning today? Will you write a poem, an article, or an editorial, perhaps? What genre makes the most sense for you?"

   - Have the group scribe post information about their learning on the students' blogs. Model how to find and embed multimedia. Invite students to embed links within their text to video clips, additional websites, and photos that describe their learning for others.
   - If you are using a learning log, have students share their learning within their individual logs. Students should still be encouraged to incorporate still images and multiple genres where appropriate.

4. Group Meeting—Groups should develop a plan for the next session. Prompt the discussion by asking the following questions: What are we still interested in learning more about? How did you use literacy to learn today?

### Session 3: Magazines and Periodicals

1. Class Meeting—Explain to students that the focus of today's class meeting is on using magazines and periodicals to navigate learning. Using models from each of the learning tubs, demonstrate how as a reader we make use of the different texts to support learning. Encourage students to use the print materials along with the digital resources to expand their learning and to answer remaining questions they might still have from last session's Group Meeting.

2. Gathering Time—Invite students use the print resources to build upon the information they have already gathered about their topics.

*(continued)*

3. Scribing Time—Have groups add to and/or revise information from the previous session to their learning log or learning blog. Circulate around the room to answer any questions.

4. Group Meeting—Ask students to review material and learning over the past two sessions. Gather student responses to the following questions: "What have we already learned about our topic that we didn't know before we began?" "What questions do we still have about our topic?" "How will we answer these questions at our next session?" "How have we been working together as a group?"

### Session 4: Books

1. Class Meeting—Explain to students that the focus of today's class meeting is on using books to navigate learning. Begin by offering a text as an example and inviting students to ask questions that the text may answer. Using these questions, model how to use a table of contents and an index to identify information and help focus reading.

2. Gathering Time—Invite students to use the print resources to build upon the information they have already gathered about their topics.

3. Scribing Time—Have groups add to and/or revise information from the previous session to their learning log or learning blog. Circulate around the room to answer any questions.

4. Group Meeting—Ask students to review material and learning over the past three sessions. Gather student responses to the following questions: "What questions do we still have about our topic?" "How will we answer these questions at our next session?"

### Session 5: Putting the Puzzle Together to Make Meaning

1. Class Meeting—Explain to students that the focus of today's class meeting is on how we synthesize the tools shared at each session to make meaning, and how we use these multimodal resources to demonstrate understanding. Demonstrate these using the learning blog. Ask students to think about audience and about how they are going to use their blogs or learning logs to create a place where others can learn about a specific topic. When looking at pictures they have included, students should ask if other viewers will understand the image; if not, they should add a caption. They should do the same with their written text.

2. Gathering Time—Ask students to identify how they are going to synthesize the information they have learned so that others can understand their topic of investigation. Circulate around the room as students work. As you meet with different groups, ask them to revisit the questions/ideas posed in the Class Meeting as a tool for organizing their ideas. Organization will vary according to the topic and task.

3. Scribing Time—Have groups revise and add to their blog or log to make the information accessible to their peers. Students should be encouraged to make this interactive. For example, you can invite students to post questions or embed links for readers of their

*(continued)*

blogs. If students are using logs, invite them to use sticky notes to offer a place for other students to respond to their work.

4. Group Meeting—Ask groups to review their work. You might pose the following questions:
   - "What did you learn about your topic during this time?"
   - "How did your work in the group support and/or interfere with your learning?"
   - "What would you do differently if you were given this opportunity again?"

These questions can be responded to individually or as part of a group discussion. If you have students, record their responses; this can be a useful assessment tool for the project.

### Session 6: An Interactive, Multimodal Learning Fair

1. Explain to students that this session is for a demonstration of learning using the multimodal tools built throughout the learning process. Students have the opportunity to interact with each of the group's blogs or logs. The nature of the interaction will be guided by the presentation of the information and the decisions the groups make about presentation. Give students 10 minutes to explore each blog or log. Ask them to talk about what they learn from each one. Before they move to the next station, they should write down or post something they learned about from the visit and something they would still like to know. Encourage them also to offer compliments to each other.

2. Have students rotate through each station either by group or individually.

### Student Assessment/Reflections

Upon completion of the experience, students can be invited to reflect on the following questions as an assessment of the project and an assessment of learning.

- "What did you learn from this experience?"
- "What tools did you use as a reader and a writer during learning clubs?"
- "What did you discover about yourself as a reader and a writer during these sessions?"
- "What did you discover about reading and writing during these sessions?"
  This reflection, as the experience itself, may be multimodal, including a podcast, a personal narrative, or a presentation to another class. You may choose to offer options or require the use of mixed media to report on the experience.
  Complete the Learning Clubs Rubric for each group. The rubric includes open categories to add information particular to your topic of study.

# Open Interest Inventory

Name: _____ Date: _____

What are you curious about? What do you wonder about? Think about what you
have been learning in your classes. What would you like to revisit? What came up in
discussions and/or readings that you didn't have the opportunity to explore further?

    We are about to begin an investigation of topics that our class is interested in
learning more about. Before we can begin, however, we need to know more about what
you want to learn. Please list topics that you are curious about below. There are two
columns. In the first column please indicate what you are interested in exploring. In the
second column, please indicate why you are interested in that topic. Topics should be
placed in order of interest.

| What I am interested in learning more about . . . | Why I am interested in this topic . . . |
|---|---|
| 1. | |
| 2. | |
| 3. | |
| 4. | |
| 5. | |

# Closed Interest Inventory

Name: _____   Date: _____

Below is a list of topics that we will be investigating in our next unit of study. Please indicate your preferences for each topic. For example, the topic that is of greatest interest is #1, and the topic of least interest is #5. Please also indicate why you feel that way about the topic.

| Topic of study | Level of interest with explanation |
| --- | --- |
|  |  |
|  |  |
|  |  |
|  |  |
|  |  |

# Learning Clubs Rubric

Group members:                    Date: _____

_____    Topic: _____

_____

_____

_____

| This blog or learning log . . . | 4 | 3 | 2 | 1 |
|---|---|---|---|---|
| Uses multiple sources to document learning | | | | |
| Was written so that it demonstrated understanding of topic | | | | |
| Has visuals that demonstrate understanding of topic | | | | |
| Synthesizes across modes and genres | | | | |
| Demonstrates successful collaboration | | | | |
| Other: | | | | |
| Other: | | | | |

4 = Excellent

3 = Good

2 = Satisfactory

1 = Unsatisfactory

**Note to readers:** It is useful to use this both as a form of self-assessment for students and as a final assessment for the teacher.

# Literacy Learning Clubs Planning Guide for Teachers

Grade level: _____

Content area: _____

Curriculum content: _____

Content-area standards: _____

How many meetings are planned? _____

When will students meet and for how long? _____
_____

What topics are available for students to choose from? _____
_____
_____

What special grouping considerations need to be made? _____
_____
_____

What types of resources (consider print and digital) are needed to support student work?
_____
_____
_____

How will student learning be assessed? _____
_____
_____

What will need to be modeled or demonstrated for students in order to scaffold their investigations? _____
_____
_____

# Focusing Session Planning Guide for Teachers

1. Meeting Number _____ of _____

2. Objective: _____

   _____

3. Standards: _____

   _____

   _____

   _____

4. Materials: _____

   _____

   _____

   _____

5. Content to be modeled/demonstrated: _____

   _____

   _____

   _____

6. Plan for students to move to literacy learning clubs: _____

   _____

   _____

   _____

   _____

7. Other considerations: _____

   _____

   _____

   _____

# Think-Aloud Planning Guide for Teachers

1. What literacy skill/strategy am I modeling/demonstrating? _____

   _____

   _____

   _____

   _____

   _____

2. How does understanding this skill or strategy help students access the content they are studying? _____

   _____

   _____

   _____

   _____

   _____

   _____

   _____

3. What resources do I need access to in order to model/demonstrate?_____

   _____

   _____

   _____

   _____

   _____

   _____

   _____

# Literacy Learning Club Meeting Planning Guide
## for Students

Preplanning guidelines to allow for a productive meeting:

1. Today at literacy learning clubs I plan to: _____

   _____

   _____

2. The resources I will likely need are: _____

   _____

   _____

3. The people I will need to work with/consult include: _____

   _____

   _____


Keeping organized during the work:

4. I am learning that: _____

   _____

   _____

5. The literacy strategies I am drawing on are: _____

   _____

   _____


Preparing for the Focusing Finish

6. The methods most useful in sharing what I have learned will be (group share, a digital document, a written narrative, etc.). This will vary according to the discipline and structure of the literacy learning club. Write your method for sharing here:

---

# Literacy Learning Club Student Exit Slip A

Name: _____ Date: _____

Complete at the end of a literacy learning club session and hand to the teacher.

- What did we learn today? _____

_____

_____

_____

_____

- How did we come to this new information? _____

_____

_____

_____

_____

- What are we still uncertain about? _____

_____

_____

_____

_____

- How will we access the information/knowledge still needed? _____

_____

_____

_____

_____

This will help you make good use of your next meeting!

# Literacy Learning Club Student Exit Slip B

Name: _____ Date: _____

Today during literacy learning clubs I:

_____ used the Internet to locate sources.

_____ read a book.

_____ posted on the class site.

_____ created a video.

_____ other.


Today I learned: _____

_____

_____

_____

_____

_____

_____

_____


Next time I plan to: _____

_____

_____

_____

_____

_____

_____

# Literacy Learning Club Preassessment Form (Sample)

**LITERACY LEARNING CLUBS TO INVESTIGATE** _Body Systems_

Name: _____     Date: _____

Please write down what you already know about the following:

1. The circulatory system _____


2. The respiratory system _____


3. The immune system _____


4. The skeletal system _____


5. The nervous system _____


6. The muscular system _____

# Literacy Learning Club Selection Form (Sample)

Name: _____

Order the areas you are most interested in learning more about below.

    1 = most interested
    6 = least interested


The circulatory system _____    _____


The respiratory system _____    _____


The immune system _____    _____


The skeletal system _____    _____


The nervous system _____    _____


The muscular system _____    _____


Secret password (e.g., your birthday or a pet's name) to be used to access our website:

_____

# Literacy Learning Club Selection Form

Name: _____

Order the areas you are most interested in learning more about below.

    1 = most interested
    6 = least interested

_____    _____

_____    _____

_____    _____

_____    _____

_____    _____

_____    _____

# Literacy Activity Inventory

This is useful for learning more about your students' literacy habits to help you inform your planning.

Age: _____     Grade: _____

We are interested in learning more about what students do inside and outside of school. Please circle the answers to some of the questions, and write your answers to others. This is anonymous.

| | Almost never | About once a month | About once a week | Almost every day |
|---|---|---|---|---|
| 1. How often do you listen to music? | 1 | 2 | 3 | 4 |
| 2. How often do you watch television? | 1 | 2 | 3 | 4 |
| 3. How often do you play outside? | 1 | 2 | 3 | 4 |
| 4. How often do you use the Internet? | 1 | 2 | 3 | 4 |

| | Always | Sometimes | Rarely | Never |
|---|---|---|---|---|
| 5. When I am researching something, I look in a book. | 1 | 2 | 3 | 4 |
| 6. When I am researching something, I read a magazine article. | 1 | 2 | 3 | 4 |
| 7. When I am researching something, I look online for information. | 1 | 2 | 3 | 4 |
| 8. I read for pleasure. | 1 | 2 | 3 | 4 |

*(continued)*

Please write your answers below (use the back if needed).

1. What does it mean to be a reader and a writer?

2. What types of texts do you read and write?

3. When do you use reading and writing outside of school or homework?

4. How do you use reading and writing in _____ (insert discipline of study) class?

A helpful professional resource for developing literacy assessments is McKenna and Stahl (2015).

# Useful Resources

## WEBSITES

- *www.weebly.com*—platform for building websites
- *www.smore.com*—interactive digital poster
- *www.classroom.google.com*—Google Classroom
- *www.edmodo.com*—tool for creating digital collaborations
- *www.literacyworldwide.org*—International Literacy Association
- *www.ncte.org*—National Council of Teachers of English
- *www.sbsciencematters.com*—Science Matters

## PROFESSIONAL ORGANIZATIONS

The following professional organizations offer a wealth of resources (many free) for teachers across the disciplines.

- *www.literacyworldwide.org*—International Literacy Association
- *www.ncte.org*—National Council of Teachers of English
- *www.nctm.org*—National Council of Teachers of Mathematics
- *www.nsta.org*—National Science Teachers Association
- *www.nextgenscience.org*—Next Generation Science Standards
- *www.socialstudies.org*—National Council for the Social Studies

## STUDENT RESOURCES

- Math for the Real World—series published by Rainbow Resource Center
- You Choose: History—series published by Capstone Press
- Open directory project for kids and teens—found at *www.dmoz.org/Kids_and_Teens/*. Search can be narrowed by discipline/topic of study.

# References

Abrams, S. S., & Russo, M. P. (2015). Layering literacies and contemporary learning. *Journal of Adolescent and Adult Literacy, 59*(2), 131–135.

Albers, P. (2012). If you think students should be critically literate—Show them how. In D. Lapp & B. Moss (Eds.), *Exemplary instruction in the middle grades* (pp. 124–144). New York: Guilford Press.

Albert, D., Chein, J., & Steinberg, L. (2013). The teenage brain: Peer influences on adolescent decision making. *Current Directions in Psychological Science, 22*(2), 114–120.

Allen, J., Schad, M., Oudekerk, B., & Chango, J. (2014). What ever happened to the "cool" kids?: Long-term sequelae of early adolescent pseudomature behavior. *Child Development, 85*(5), 1866–1880.

Almasi, J. F., & Garas-York, K. (2009). Comprehension and peer discussion. In S. Israel & G. G. Duffy (Eds.), *Handbook of research on reading comprehension* (pp. 470–493). Mahwah, NJ: Erlbaum.

Alvermann, D. (2013). Popular culture and literacy practices. In M. L. Kamil, P. D. Pearson, E. B. Moje, & P. Afflerbach (Eds.), *Handbook of reading research* (Vol. 4, pp. 541–560). New York: Routledge.

Anderman, E., Griesinger, T., & Westerfield, G. (1998). Motivation and cheating during early adolescence. *Journal of Educational Psychology, 90*(1), 84–93.

Anders, P. L., & Pritchard, T. G. (1993). Integrated language curriculum and instruction for the middle grades. *Elementary School Journal, 93*, 611–624.

Anderson, J., & Rainie, L. (2014). Digital life in 2025. PEW Research Center. Retrieved from *www.pewinternet.org/files/2014/03/PIP_Report_Future_of_the_Internet_Predictions_031114.pdf*.

Atwell, N. (2014). *In the middle: New understandings about writing, reading, and learning* (3rd ed.). Portsmouth, NH: Heinemann.

Baer, J., & Kaufman, J. (1998). Gender differences in creativity. *Journal of Creative Behavior, 42*(2), 75–105.

Bakhtin, M. M. (1981). From the prehistory of novelistic discourse (C. Emerson & M. Holquist, Trans.). In M. Holquist (Ed.), *The dialogic imagination* (pp. 41–83). Austin: University of Texas Press.

Bean, R. (2015). *The reading specialist: Leadership and coaching for the classroom, school and community* (3rd ed.). New York: Guilford Press.

Bean, T. W., Bean, S. K., & Bean, K. F. (1999). Intergenerational conversations and two adolescents' multiple literacies: Implications for redefining content area literacy. *Journal of Adolescent and Adult Literacy, 42,* 438–448.

Beane, J. A., & Brodhagen, B. (2001). Teaching in middle schools. In V. Richardson (Ed.), *Handbook of research on teaching* (pp. 1157–1175). Washington, DC: American Educational Research Association.

Biancarosa, G., & Snow, C. E. (2004). *Reading next—A vision for action and research in middle and high school literacy: A report from Carnegie Corporation of New York.* Washington, DC: Alliance for Excellent Education.

Blanchard, J. S., & Samuels, S. J. (2015). Common core state standards and multiple-source reading comprehension. In P. D. Pearson & E. H. Hiebert (Eds.), *Research based practices for teaching Common Core Literacy* (pp. 93–106). New York: Teachers College Press.

Broomhead, P. (2010). (Re)imagining literacies for music classrooms. In R. J. Draper, P. Broomhead, A. Peterson Jensen, J. Nokes, & D. Siebert (Eds.), *(Re)imagining content-area literacy instruction* (pp. 69–81). New York: Teachers College Press

Bulgar, S. (2003) Children's sense-making of division of fractions. *Journal of Mathematical Behaviors, 22*(3), 319–334.

Casey, H. (2012a). Multimodal learning clubs. *Middle School Journal, 44,* 39–48.

Casey, H. (2012b). Learning clubs: A framework for using literacy to learn. *Journal of Reading Education, 38*(1), 31–37.

Casey, H. (2012c). If you value collaboration-hold students accountable for collaborative group work. In D. Lapp & B. Moss (Eds.), *Exemplary instruction in the middle grades: Teaching that supports engagement and rigorous earning* (pp. 224–242). New York: Guilford Press.

Casey, H. (2015). Moving beyond print: What do new literacies mean for teacher education? *The Reading Professor, 37*(1), 23–28.

Casey, H., Kawalek, K., Young, K., & Harris, N. (2016). *Literacy PD that works: An action plan for change.* Paper presented at the annual conference of the International Literacy Association, Boston.

Casey, H., Lenski, S., & Hryniuk-Adamov, C. (Eds.). (2014/2015). *Literacy practices that adolescents deserve: An IRA E-ssentials series.* Newark, DE: International Reading Association. Retrieved from *www.literacyworldwide.org/get-resources/ila-e-ssentials*.

Casey, H., Lenski, S., & Hryniuk-Adamov, C. (2014). Access to a wide variety of print and nonprint materials. In H. Casey, S. Lenski, & C. Hryniuk-Adamov (Eds.), *Literacy practices that adolescents deserve: An IRA E-ssentials series.* Newark, DE:

International Literacy Association. Retrieved from *www.literacyworldwide.org/get-resources/ila-e-ssentials/8059*.

Central New Jersey YMCA announcement (2016). *Junior InVision*. Bridgewater, NJ: Author.

Chall, J. S., Jacobs, V. A., & Baldwin, L. E. (1990). *The reading crisis: Why poor children fall behind*. Cambridge, MA: Harvard University Press.

Charles, R. I. (2005). Big ideas and understandings as the foundation for elementary and middle school mathematics. *Journal of Mathematics Education Leadership, 7*(3), 9–24.

Coiro, J., Knoble, M., Lankshear, C., & Leu, D. J. (Eds.). (2008). *Handbook of research on new literacies*. Mahwah, NJ: Erlbaum.

Dalhouse, D. W., Dalhouse, A. D., & Mitchell, D. (1997). Development of a literature based middle school reading program: Insights gained. *Journal of Adolescent and Adult Literacy, 40*, 362–370.

Daniels, H. (2002). *Literature circles: Voice and choice in book clubs and reading groups*. Portland, ME: Stenhouse.

Draper, R., Broomhead, P., Jensen, A. P., Nokes, J., & Siebert, D. (Eds.). (2010). *(Re)imagining content-area literacy instruction*. New York: Teachers College Press.

Draper, S. M. (2010). *Out of my mind*. New York: Atheneum.

Duke, N. (2014). *Inside information: Developing powerful readers and writers of informational text through project-based instruction*. New York: Scholastic.

Dunkerly, J., & Bean, T. (2014). Using critical literacy to promote human rights and civic engagement. In H. Casey, S. Lenski, & C. Hryniuk-Adamov (Eds.), *Literacy practices that adolescents deserve: An IRA E-ssentials series*. Newark, DE: International Literacy Association. Retrieved from *www.literacyworldwide.org/get-resources/ila-e-ssentials/8058*.

Ebert, C. (2015). Laurence Steinberg: "Age of opportunity: Lessons from the new science of adolescence" [Review]. *Journal of Youth and Adolescence, 44*(8), 1652–1655.

Fang, Z. (2012). Language correlates of disciplinary literacy. *Topics in Language Disorders, 32*, 19–34.

Fisher, D., & Frey, N. (2008). *Better learning through structured teaching: A framework for the gradual release of responsibility*. Alexandria, VA: Association for Supervision and Curriculum Development.

Fisher, D., & Frey, N. (2015). *Improving adolescent literacy: Content area strategies at work*. New York: Pearson.

Fitchett, P., Heafner, T., & VanFossen, P. (2014). An analysis of time prioritization for social studies in elementary classrooms. *Journal of Curriculum and Instruction, 8*, 7–35.

Fleming, L. (2015). *Worlds of making: Best practices for makerspace for your school*. Thousand Oaks, CA: Corwin Press.

Freire, P., & Macedo, D. (1987). *Reading the word and the world*. New York: Praeger.

Gallagher, K. (2009). *Readicide: How schools are killing reading and what you can do about it*. Portland, ME: Stenhouse.

Garrett, T. (2014). *Classroom management: The essentials*. New York: Teachers College Press.

Guthrie, J. T. (2008). *Engaging adolescents in reading.* Thousand Oaks, CA: Corwin Press.

Guthrie, J. T. (2015). Growth of motivations for cognitive processes of reading. In P. D. Pearson & E. H. Hiebert (Eds.), *Research based practices for teaching Common Core Literacy* (pp. 107–122). New York: Teachers College Press.

Guthrie, J. T., Wigfield, A., & Klauda, S. L. (2012). Adolescents' engagement in academic literacy (Report No. 7). Retrieved May 11, 2016, from *www.corilearning.com/research-publications.*

Harper, H., Bean, T. W., & Dunkerly, J. (2010). Cosmopolitanism, globalization and the field of adolescent literacy. *Canadian and International Education/Education Canadienne et international, 39*(3), 1–13.

Harvey, S., & Daniels, H. (2015). *Comprehension and collaboration: Inquiry circles for curiosity, engagement and understanding.* Portsmouth, NH: Heinemann.

Hinchman, K., & Sherindan-Thomas, H. (Eds.). (2014). *Best practices in adolescent literacy instruction* (2nd ed.). New York: Guilford Press.

Hunt, L. M. (2015). *Fish in a tree.* New York: Penguin.

International Literacy Association. (2016). *Frameworks for literacy education reform* [White paper]. Newark, DE: Author.

International Reading Association. (2009). *New literacies and 21st-century technologies: A position statement of the International Reading Association.* Newark, DE: Author.

International Reading Association. (2012). *Adolescent literacy* (Position statement, Rev. 2012 ed.). Newark, DE: Author.

Ippoliti, J., Dobbs, C., Charner-Laird, M., & Lawrence, J. (2016). Delicate layers of learning: Achieving disciplinary literacy requires continuous, collaborative adjustment. *JSD Learning Forward, 37*(2), 34–38.

Ivey, G., & Broaddus, K. (2000). Tailoring the fit: Reading instruction and middle school readers. *The Reading Teacher, 54,* 68–78.

Ivey, G., & Fisher, D. (2007). *Creating literacy-rich schools for adolescents.* Alexandria, VA: ASCD.

Jenkins, H., & Kelley, W. (2013). *Reading in a participatory culture.* New York: Teachers College Press: National Writing Project.

Jensen, A. P., Asay, D. L., & Gray, S. (2010). (Re)imagining literacies for visual arts classrooms. In R. J. Draper, P. Broomhead, A. Peterson Jensen, J. Nokes, & D. Siebert (Eds.), *(Re)imagining content-area literacy instruction* (pp. 144–158). New York: Teachers College Press.

Johnson, L., Adams Becker, S., Estrada, V., & Freeman, A. (2015). *NMC Horizon Report: 2015 K–12 edition.* Austin, TX: New Media Consortium.

Juliani, A. J. (2014). *Inquiry and innovation in the classroom: Using 20% time, genius hour, and PBL to drive student success.* London: Routledge.

Juvonen, J., Vi-Nhuan, L., Kaganoff, T., Augustine, C., & Constant, L. (2004). *Focus on the wonder years: Challenges facing the American middle school.* Santa Monica, CA: RAND Corp.

Keene, E. O., & Zimmermann, S. (2007). *Mosaic of thought: The power of comprehension strategy instruction* (2nd ed.). Portsmouth, NH: Heinemann.

Kittle, P. (2013). *Book love: Developing depth, stamina, and passion in adolescent readers.* Portsmouth, NH: Heinemann.

Kress, G. (2010). *Multimodality: A social semiotic approach to contemporary communication.* New York: Routledge.

Lehman, C., & Roberts, K. (2014). *Falling in love with close reading: Lessons for analyzing texts—and life.* Portsmouth, NH: Heinemann.

Lenhart, A. (2015). Teen, social media and technology overview 2015. Pew Research Report. Retrieved from *www.pewinternet.org/files/2015/04/PI_TeensandTech_Update 2015_0409151.pdf.*

Leu, D. J., Forzani, E., Burlingame, C., Kulikowich, J., Sedransk, N., Coiro, J., et al. (2013). The new literacies of online research and comprehension: Assessing and preparing students for the 21st century with Common Core State Standards. In S. B. Neuman & L. B. Gambrell (Eds.), C. Massey (Assoc. Ed.), *Reading instruction in the age of Common Core Standards* (pp. 219–236). Newark, DE: International Reading Association.

Leu, D. J., Forzani, E., Rhoads, C., Maykel, C., Kennedy, C., & Timbrell, N. (2015). The new literacies of online research and comprehension: Rethinking the reading achievement gap. *Reading Research Quarterly, 50*(1), 37–59.

Leu, D. J., Zawilinski, L., Forzani, E., & Timbrell, N. (2014). Best practices in new literacies and the new literacies of online research and comprehension. In L. B. Gambrell & L. M. Morrow (Eds.), *Best practices in literacy instruction* (5th ed., pp. 343–364). New York: Guilford Press.

Levy, S. (2013, March). Big ideas: Google's Larry Page and the gospel of 10x. *Wired.* Retrieved from *www.wired.co.uk/article/a-healthy-disregard-for-the-impossible.*

Ley, T., Schaer, B., & Dismukes, B. (1994). Longitudinal study of the reading attitudes and behaviors of middle school students. *Reading Psychology, 15,* 11–38.

Lieberman, A., & Miller, L. (2014). Teachers as professionals: Evolving definitions of staff development. In L. E. Martin, S. Kragler, D. J. Quatroche, & K. L. Bauserman (Eds.), *Handbook of professional development in education: Successful models and practices, PreK–12* (pp. 3–21). New York: Guilford Press.

Lima, M., & Oakes, W. (2013). *Service-learning: Engineering in your community.* New York: Oxford University Press.

Lord, C. (2006). *Rules.* New York: Scholastic.

Madden, M., Lenhart, A., Duggan, M., Cortesi, S., & Gasser, U. (2013). Teens and technology. Pew Research Report. Retrieved from *www.pewinternet.org/2013/03/13/teens-and-technology-2013.*

McKenna, M., & Stahl, K. A. D. (2015). *Assessment for reading instruction.* New York: Guilford Press.

Mickler, M. J., & Irvin, J. (2015). Implementing a schoolwide literacy action plan for adolescents. In H. Casey, S. Lenski, & C. Hryniuk-Adamov (Eds.), *Literacy practices that adolescents deserve: An IRA E-ssentials series.* Newark, DE: International Literacy Association. Retrieved from *www.literacyworldwide.org/get-resources/ila-e-ssentials/8071.*

Miller, D., & Anderson, J. (2009). *The book whisperer: Awakening the inner reader in every child.* San Francisco: Jossey-Bass.

Miller, D., & Kelley, S. (2013). *Reading in the wild: The book whisperer's keys to cultivating lifelong reading habits.* San Francisco: Jossey-Bass.

Moje, E., Dillon, D., & O'Brien, D. (2000). Reexamining roles of learner, text and context in secondary literacy. *Journal of Educational Research, 93,* 165–180.

Morrow, L., Reutzel, D., & Casey, H. (2014). Organization and management of language arts teaching. In C. M. Everston & C. S. Weinstein (Eds.), *Handbook of classroom management research, practice, and contemporary issues* (pp. 559–582). New York: Routledge.

National Assessment of Educational Progress. (2010). Civics assessment. Retrieved from *www.nationsreportcard.gov/civics_2010/about_civics.aspx.*

National Association for Music Education. (2014). *2014 music standards.* Reston, VA: Author. Retrieved from *www.nafme.org.*

National Business Education Association (2007). *National standards for business education.* Reston, VA: Author. Retrieved from *www.nbea.org.*

National Coalition for Core Arts Standards. (2014) *National core arts standards.* Dover, DE: Author. Retrieved from *www.nationalartsstandards.org.*

National Council for the Social Studies. (n.d.). About National Council for the Social Studies. Retrieved from *www.socialstudies.org/about.*

National Council of Teachers of English. (2013). The NCTE definition of 21st century literacies. Position Statement. Retrieved from *www.ncte.org/positions/statements/21stcentdefinition.*

National Council of Teachers of Mathematics. (2013). Supporting the Common Core State Standards for Mathematics. Position statement. Retrieved from *www.nctm.org/ccssmposition.*

National Council of Teachers of Mathematics. (2014). Procedural fluency in mathematics. Position statement. Retrieved from *www.nctm.org/Standards-and-Positions/Position-Statements/Procedural-Fluency-in-Mathematics.*

National Governors Association Center for Best Practices & Council of Chief State School Officers. (2010). *Common Core State Standards for English language arts and literacy in history/social studies, science, and technical subjects.* Washington, DC: Author. Retrieved from *www.corestandards.org/the-standards.*

National Middle School Association. (2010). *This we believe* (4th ed.). Westerville, OH: Association for Middle Level Education.

National Research Council. (2012). *A framework for K–12 science education: Practices, crosscutting concepts, and core ideas.* Washington, DC: National Academies Press.

National Writing Project. (2016). Letters to the next president. Retrieved from *www.letters2president.org.*

NGSS Lead States. (2013). *Next generation science standards: For states, by states.* Washington, DC: National Academies Press.

Nokes, J. (2010). (Re)imagining literacies for history classrooms. In R. J. Draper, P.

Broomhead, A. Peterson Jensen, J. Nokes, & D. Siebert (Eds.), (Re)imagining content-area literacy instruction (pp. 54–68). New York: Teachers College Press.

Norris, A. (2014). Make-her-spaces as hybrid places: Designing and resisting self-construction in urban classrooms. Equity and Excellence in Education, 47(1), 63–77.

O'Byrne, W. I., & Pytash, K. E. (2015). Hybrid and blended learning. Journal of Adolescent and Adult Literacy, 59(2), 137–140.

Palacio, R. J. (2012). Wonder. New York: Knopf.

Parsons, S. A., Malloy, J. A., Parsons, A. W., & Burrowbridge, S. C. (2015). Students' engagement in literacy tasks. The Reading Teacher, 69(2), 223–231.

Pearson, P. D., & Gallagher, G. (1983). The gradual release of responsibility model of instruction. Contemporary Educational Psychology, 8, 112–123.

Prensky, M. (2001). Digital natives, digital immigrants. On the Horizon, 9(5). Retrieved from www.marcprensky.com/writing/Prensky%20%20Digital%20Natives,%20Digital%20Immigrants%20-%20Part1.pdf.

Pressley, M., & Allington, R. L. (2015). Reading instruction that works: The case for balanced teaching (4th ed.). New York: Guilford Press.

Raum, E. (2016). The revolutionary war: An interactive history adventure (you choose: History). Mankato, MN: Capstone.

Rief, L. (2014). Read, write, teach: Choice and challenge in the reading–writing workshop. Portsmouth, NH: Heinemann.

Schoenbach, R., Greenleaf, C., & Murphy, L. (2012). Reading for understanding: How reading apprenticeship improves disciplinary learning in secondary and college classrooms (2nd ed.). San Francisco: Jossey-Bass.

Shanahan, C. (2015). Disciplinary literacy strategies in content area classes. In H. Casey, S. Lenski, & C. Hryniuk-Adamov (Eds.), Literacy practices that adolescents deserve: An IRA E-ssentials series. Newark, DE: International Reading Association. Retrieved from www.literacyworldwide.org/get-resources/ila-e-ssentials/8069.

Shanahan, C., Shanahan, T., & Misischia, C. (2011). Analysis of expert readers in three disciplines: History, mathematics, and chemistry. Journal of Literacy Research, 43(4), 393–429.

Shaw, L. A., Amsel, E., & Schillo, J. (2011). Risk taking in late adolescence: Relations between sociomoral reasoning, risk stance, and behavior. Journal of Research on Adolescence, 21(4), 881–894.

Siebert, D., & Hendrickson, S. (2010). (Re)imagining literacies for mathematics classrooms. In R. J. Draper, P. Broomhead, A. Peterson Jensen, J. Nokes, & D. Siebert (Eds.), (Re)imagining content-area literacy instruction (pp. 20–39). New York: Teachers College Press.

Siegel, M. (2012). New times for multimodality?: Confronting the accountability culture. Journal of Adolescent and Adult Literacy, 55, 671–680.

Skinner, K., Pearce, D. L., & Barrera, E. S. (2016). Literacy difficulties of elementary students when solving mathematical word problems. Literacy Practice and Research, 41(2), 29–36.

Smagorinsky, P. (2015). Disciplinary literacy in English language arts. *Journal of Adolescent and Adult Literacy, 59*(2), 141–146.

Smith, F. (1987). *Joining the literacy club: Further essays into education.* Portsmouth, NH: Heinemann.

Society of Health and Physical Educators. (2013). *National PE standards.* Reston, VA: SHAPE America. Retrieved from *www.shapeamerica.org.*

Spencer, H. (1860). *Education: Intellectual, moral, and physical* (pp. 21–96). New York: Appleton. Retrieved from *http://dx.doi.org/10.1037/12158–001.*

Spinelli, J. (2002). *Loser.* New York: Harper Trophy.

Springen, K. (2007, February). Fourth grade slump. *Newsweek.*

Strauss, S., & Irvin, J. (2000, September). Exemplary literacy learning programs. *Middle School Journal,* 3–5.

The Math PLaCe. Real-world applications of linear functions. Retrieved from *http://teacherweb.com/NC/AlgebraKNECT/HomerSpring/apt3.aspx.*

Tomlinson, C. (2001). *Differentiation of instruction in the mixed ability classroom.* Alexandria, VA: ASCD.

Tovani, C. (2011). *So what do they really know?: Assessment that informs teaching and learning.* Portland, ME: Stenhouse.

Turner, K. H., & Hicks, T. (2015). *Connected reading: Teaching adolescent readers in a digital world.* Urbana, IL: NCTE.

Tryphon, A., & Vonèche, J. (Eds.). (1996). *Piaget Vygotsky: The social genesis of thought.* New York: Psychology Press.

Underwood, M. K., & Faris, R. (2015). #Being thirteen: Social media and the hidden world of young adolescents' peer culture. CNN Anderson Cooper 360 collaboration/ production. Retrieved from *https://assets.documentcloud.org/documents/2448422/being-13-report.pdf.*

Vygotsky, L. (1978). *Mind in society* (M. Cole, V. John-Steiner, S. Scribner, & E. Souberman, Eds.). Cambridge, MA: Harvard University Press.

Vygotsky, L. (1986). *Thought and language* (A. Kozulin, Ed.). Cambridge, MA: MIT Press.

Walsh, R. (2016). *A parent's guide to public education in the 21st century: Navigating education reform to get the best education for my child.* New York: Garn Press.

# Index

*Note*: f following a page number indicates a figure; t indicates a table.